A STUDENT'S GUIDE TO UNIVERSITY AND LEARNING

CONNOR WHITELEY

No part of this book may be reproduced in any form or by any electronic or mechanical means. Including information storage, and retrieval systems, without written permission from the author except for the use of brief quotations in a book review.

This book is NOT legal, professional, medical, financial or any type of official advice.

Any questions about the book, rights licensing, or to contact the author, please email connorwhiteley@connorwhiteley.net

Copyright © 2023 CONNOR WHITELEY

All rights reserved.

DEDICATION
Thank you to all my readers without you I couldn't do what I love.

INTRODUCTION

When it comes to learning and exams and more at university, there is so much that is just assumed. Universities just assume that you know exactly how to revise, study and do well in coursework.

In addition, universities just assume that you know the benefits of work experience, how to find a part-time job and so much more.

However, it doesn't actually have to be this way, because in this book you'll learn a lot about university, how to learn about university and so much more that will really help you in the future.

<u>What Will This Book Cover?</u>

For the sake of ease and in an effort to be as helpful as possible, this book is divided up into six main sections with each focusing on a different but very interesting aspect of university life.

- General Learning Tips

This section covers things like minimising distractions, online learning and revision tips.

- Exams

This is one of the most important sections because it covers important topics like exam preparation, stress and more great chapters that help you to do well.

- Coursework

This is definitely a section I wish I had when I started university because it covers things like time management, group projects and presentations.

As well as if you're anything like me then chances are you hate group projects and presentations. This book gives you some critical tips to help you cope better with these pieces of coursework.

- Social Tips For University

This is a great section for people who are nervous about trying to make friends at university and not sure how to find your people.

It's only in the past year and a bit that I'm realising how critical this information was to my own university life, as someone who isn't naturally extroverted and social.

- The Christmas Break

Now this section might not sound that exciting at first but lots of readers (because these chapters are based on the blog posts I wrote for the e-learning platform Active Class) have found these posts very useful and surprising.

So definitely check them out.

- Work Experience, Placements and Jobs

The final section is probably one of the most important sections in the entire book, because we all hear how tough it is for graduates to get a job at university. Since whilst degrees are very useful and invaluable, it is your employability and the extra things you do that help you to stand out in the job market.

And for psychology that is especially true, so this final section really helps you to understand how to boost your employability for the future.

<u>Who Is This Book For?</u>

Whilst this engaging, easy-to-understand book is mainly designed for psychology students, whether it is people already at university or those thinking of going to university, this book is great for everyone.

Since whilst the book focuses on psychology degrees, because that is my own experience and background, it is still jam-packed with useful information that you're bound to find useful regardless of the subject of your degree.

<u>Who Am I?</u>

Personally I always like to know who writes the nonfiction I read, so I know it's coming from a good source.

Therefore, in case you are like me, I am Connor Whiteley. An author of over 30 psychology books, and the host of The Psychology World Podcast, available on all major podcast apps and YouTube, where each week we talk about a new fascinating area of psychology and the latest psychology news.

However, most importantly for this book at least, I am a psychology student at the University Of Kent, England studying Psychology With Clinical Psychology and A Placement Year.

In other words, I focus on the mental health side of psychology in my final year.

So now we know more about each other, let's dive into the great world of learning more about university.

PART ONE: GENERAL LEARNING TIPS

5 REVISION TECHNIQUES FOR UNIVERSITY STUDENTS

I decided to kick off this book by starting to look at general learning tips and tricks before moving onto the focused topics exams and coursework and everything else that the book looks at.

And I can't think of a better way to start than looking at arguably one of the most important things about university life.

Revision.

As well as this is a very nice way and easy to ease into the rest of the book before we get to more extremely specific and focused things that sadly universities and others don't tell you.

Enjoy!

<u>5 Revision Techniques For University Students</u>

There are millions of resources, blog posts and videos on revision techniques for students. Some of them are great. Some of them are not. But the reason why you should read this blog post is because this is my take on the topic and as with all of my posts, you get some personal examples, lessons learnt and a wonderfully voice-y post. That actually makes reading it interesting! So keep reading if you want to learn about revision techniques for university students!

Why Are Revision techniques Important?

Personally I always find this to be an important reminder because too much of the time I simply dive into revision without thinking what's best for me. Since some topics I learn best revising one way. Other topics I learn best revising another way.

This is why revision techniques are so important. It's a great idea to be aware of a wide range of them so you have plenty of techniques at your fingertips. This allows you to try different things until you find something that works for you.

Reading and Watching Lectures

We're definitely starting off with the basics here, but rereading material and watching your lectures can be a great way to start revising. Reading will allow you to refresh all the detail that your lectures couldn't go into, and watching your lectures allows you to remember some of the key principles explained in your lecturers' words.

That really can be critical sometimes, because as we all know, textbooks are… textbooks and they're filled with some very horrible definitions and explanations. But our lecturers are professionals who have been working with students long enough to know how best to explain things.

In addition, rewatching lectures and rereading can be a great way to find out what you need to focus on. Since if you're reading along thinking you remember this all, then you find a section you have no memory of. Guess what, that's a section you really need to focus on.

That may have happened to me once or twice.

Overall, watching lectures and rereading your textbooks can be a great place to start. But personally I really wouldn't use this as your only method.

<u>Getting People To Quiz You</u>

There are two horrifically underrated revision techniques I'll tell you about in this post and this is one of them.

Getting people to quiz you is brilliant for exams that require you to write down answers in short-answered questions or multiple-choice questions. Due to if you're able to explain to someone about a concept clearly, concisely and in an easy-to-understand way, then you should do good on your exam.

Additionally, it's even better if you can tell someone who doesn't do the same subject as you because then you really have to explain it well.

Therefore, you can get your friends, family and maybe your study group if you have one, to quiz you and test your knowledge.

I've found being quizzed very helpful in the past, because not only does it help you understand things better. But it really makes you concentrate more because you don't want to look silly or make a massive mistake when someone is quizzing you.

Basically you don't want to look like a fool, so you revise better to make sure that doesn't happen!

<u>Practising Writing Essays</u>

I seriously was in two minds about giving out this revision technique because its effectiveness really depends on your exams.

Personally I found this extremely helpful before I came to university when I was doing the International Baccalaureate, because the exam questions were so predictable.

However, at university, I haven't done this revision technique at all because you can't predict the exam question at all. But if you do a degree where the question are predictable or you can make them up and they would still be useful, then this can be very effective.

As a result, you're practising your academic writing, testing if you know everything you would need for an essay and seeing if there are any more citations and references that you need.

On the other hand, there are some exams where you are given the essay question ahead of your exams. I have one of them in my final year, and of course I will be doing this then for the reasons above, and another one.

Practising writing essays ahead of time can really help you focus on the other citations you need. Because as we all know, every single little thing in academic writing must be referenced, no matter how small a detail, a point or anything, it all has to be referenced. Which isn't bad per se, it is just a pain.

Therefore, by practising ahead of time, it allows you to see what other citations and references you need to get ahead of your exam.

<u>YouTube Videos</u>

The other seriously underrated revision technique is watching YouTube videos, because there is so much content out there in the world that you can learn a lot for your revision. As well as the good thing about videos is you have someone guiding you through it and they often tend to explain it better than academics.

Which is the nice thing about looking beyond the normal textbooks, lectures and other academic resources when it comes to revision. Since at no fault of their own, sometimes academics only explain things in the most complicated academic terms, because they have to. After researching, writing up reports and everything else they do, sometimes it's hard for academics to remember they are talking to students and not professionals.

Therefore, if you're stuck on a topic, I would just search YouTube and just find some videos on the topic.

Personally, this is exactly how I learnt most of SPSS, and it's probably how I'll learn R when I go into my final year. Due to I was coming up one of my computing exams and statistics, got the checklist of what I was meant to know and then I realised that because the Teaching Assistants (or whatever their title is) had explained it so strangely because they had been Masters of SPSS for over five years. I realised I hadn't absorbed the information and the lecture notes, PowerPoints and lectures weren't helping.

Hence I went onto YouTube, watched some very easy to understand videos and did really well on my exam.

So again, it's always great to step out of the academic ecosystem.

<u>Memorising Content</u>

Now I wanted to have this technique as the last one because this is the most research support technique. As well as whilst I'll include two references so you can read more about this if you are so inclined, I'll explain want why memorising your revision material is the best method in layman terms.

So when we "remember" things we are actually retrieving information that is stored in our memory, and these retrieval paths can be thought of as roads. A road from our memory to the front of our brain where we consciously remember things. (If any psychology people are reading this just take some deep breaths at this oversimplification)

In addition, like all roads the more a road is used the better it is, because a motorway might get put it to make the transport link stronger.

And you can think of revision like this, because the more you revise and remember a piece of information, the stronger this link gets. This makes it easier for you to get that piece of information from your memory to the front of your brain where we "remember" it.

Therefore, in terms of revision, the easiest way to use this technique is to simply read a paragraph, cover it up and try to recall what you've read. This way you're learning the information and it's getting stored in your memory, but you're making sure you can recall it when you need to. Hence you're making the retrieval path (road) stronger between your memory and the front of your brain.

Moreover, you can incorporate this technique (or at least the principles) with the other ones I've given you. For example, you could practice with a friend and other people doing the same exam as you and test each other on how much do you both remember of a given passage.

It's all about being aware of what you can do, and then getting creative to develop revision techniques that work for you.

Conclusion:

As I mentioned at the beginning of the post, there are plenty of resources on this area, so you might want to check them out for even more resources.

But I really hope at the end of this post, you've now got a lot more techniques with real-world examples on how to revise.

Therefore, I wish you the best of luck with your

revision, exams and the rest of your university experience.

Reference For How memorising Content Works Better:

Whiteley, C. (2021). *Cognitive Psychology: A Guide to Neuropsychology, Neuroscience and Cognitive Psychology*. CGD Publishing.

Ward, J. (2015). *The student's guide to cognitive neuroscience*. psychology press.

5 THINGS YOU NEED TO MASTER ONLINE LEARNING

If you're read the first book in the series *How Does University Work?* Then you might remember the chapter talking about online university being here to stay and why that isn't a bad thing.

Therefore, this is a critical chapter if you do online learning as this will really help you get the best possible results.

Enjoy!

5 Things You Need To Master Online Learning For University Students

The COVID-19 pandemic changed the way universities taught their courses with lectures and seminars moving online. But this change to online learning has bought new challenges to student's success. In this blog post, you're going to learn 5 tips to help you master online learning from a student who's been doing online learning for over a year.

Scheduling:

At first, I thought this is a very weird tip to offer but I encourage you to master scheduling because it makes online learning a lot easier. Because the main problem with online learning is there are no set times for anything.

In my experience, the readings and the lectures were given ahead of time and the only truly scheduled thing was my psychology statistics. Meaning I had a lot of free time to do the reading and watch the lectures.

This is where scheduling becomes important because if you can't schedule your time properly. Then you will probably struggle to watch all the lectures, do the readings and do any assignments or coursework that you need to do. Leading to you most probably feeling overwhelmed. We don't want this.

Scheduling is very important to master for online learning.

Minimising Distractions

I highly recommend the other post on the blog about how to minimise distractions. But to connect it to online learning, the better you are at minimising these distractions the better your online learning experience will be. Because you'll be able to focus more and you should be able to learn more.

From my experience, I definitely found the fewer distractions I had around me the better I found the online learning. Due to I was able to dive into the topic and get deep into it without a distraction breaking my concentration and pulling me away from the topic.

We've all been there when we want to learn something but there are so many distractions, we end up giving up.

You don't want that for your online learning!

Productivity:

Leading on from the last point, with our distractions minimised it should allow us to be more productive and this is just critical for online learning.

As a result, another problem with being at home and doing online learning is we're at home and it's all too easy to be distracted and not be productive. But this can catch you out because if you don't make a productive use of your time. You'll fall behind, your readings will pile up and your lectures don't get watched.

In my university year, I've seen way too many people panic a few weeks before the exams because they didn't make a productive use of their time, and now they have hundreds of pages to read.

Don't do this to yourself!

Overall, master being productive and keeping on top of your online learning so you don't end up in a panic before the exams!

Time Management:

I've probably touched on this in previous blog posts but time management links to productivity and scheduling. Yet it does deserve its own section because of how important it is.

Not only because it allows you to stay on top of your online learning but because it means you can do other things besides your online learning.

Since we all know if you don't have fun, relax, have breaks, go out with friends, etc. then this leads to burnout and a decrease in your mental health. We don't want that!

Therefore, what time management allows you to do is it means you can allocate or think about how much time your online learning will take. Giving you a rough idea how much free time you have.

I made very good use of this because I had an extremely hard rule about my online learning. Fridays and Saturdays are mine. And in all honesty, Wednesdays and Thursdays were mine too. Unless I was doing coursework or assignments.

My time management skills allowed me to understand and be productive on Sundays, Mondays and Tuesdays so I could have the rest of the week effectively off.

Of course, your course will have different requirements and your lifestyle will be different to mine. You might want to work different days and different hours.

But the entire point of this section is to inspire you that time management allows you to be flexible and have a life outside of your online learning. Needless to say, it's important to master.

<u>Active Class</u>

The final thing I recommend you master is

Active Class because this is a great piece of software that allows you to do so much to help your online learning. For example, it helps with scheduling, seeing your timetable and planning around it and it has a lot of other features.

Whilst I didn't have access to Active Class during my studies, I wish I had. It could have saved me a bit of time each week. So I do recommend it.

Conclusion:

I don't think online learning is going anywhere and there are benefits, but there are drawbacks too.

After reading this blog post, I hope you have a better understanding of the things you should master to help your learning.

I wish you the best of luck.

Have a great day!

3 TIPS TO REDUCE DISTRACTIONS ONLINE LEARNING

To finish this section on general learning lips and online learning, we need to look at the all important topic of distractions because whether you do online or in-person learning. There will be times when you get distracted and for the sake of your education you definitely need to learn how to deal with them.

And I know what you're thinking, distractions are rare as well as you only have one or two distractions at a time. That might sound okay but as you'll see in the rest of this chapter, it is about the distractions damaging your learning over time.

That's why it's critical to look at this topic.

3 Tips To Reduce Distractions During Online Learning

Even before the pandemic started online learning has been a very popular option for education, both formal and informal. Personally, I love online learning for various topics because it's easy and often a lot more practical than in-person learning.

However, let's face it. In this digital, modern world, there are plenty of distractions that take our focus away from our learning and onto other things we shouldn't be focusing on. I know I tend to check emails after a while when I'm meant to be watching a lecture.

So how do we reduce these distractions?

3 Tips To Reduce Distractions

Choose Your Study Place Carefully

Thankfully most places nowadays have good Wi-Fi so most places are very good options as places to study whilst online. But you need to pick your study place carefully because you want to minimize distractions and encourage yourself to focus.

For example, if you love to talk to other people then maybe a busy coffee shop isn't a good place for you so maybe a quiet library or your quiet room is better.

Equally, if you hate the silence and need some background noise to focus then a busy coffee shop would be perfect for you.

The entire point of this tip is to get you to think about what you need to focus so you can make adjustments, reduce temptation and increase your focus.

Pick Your Study Buddies Wisely

Personally, I've never really liked the idea of study buddies because I do find other people distracting and the idea of being in a group in silence whilst studying makes me shake my head. I really wouldn't like to be in that situation.

However, for some people it does help because the person has more accountability and if you're stuck then you can ask for help. Which is always good.

Also linking this to online learning, I know lots of my friends have got together at the library, in their houses and in other places to watch lectures together. As well as this applies to online group work because I've had to do a lot of these during the Pandemic, and to be honest I don't see this online group work decreasing anytime soon.

On the other hand, if you've ever worked in a group (online or off) before then you can probably remember at least a couple of times when there's been one person who distracts the entire group. Either with silly comments, talking off topic and generally being annoying.

This is why it's critical for you to pick your study buddies wisely because if you don't then you risk becoming distracted and your academic performance could decrease.

On the whole, the key with this tip is to set time aside for studying and general talking with friends that want to help you achieve your goals of doing well in your learning. This is what people high in self-regulation do to be successful in study groups. (VanDellen et al, 2015)

Protect Yourself From Distractions

I know this tip is probably the most overrated and over-said but it is very true and so few people listen to this advice.

If you really want to reduce distractions during your online learning, you have to make sure you try to protect yourself. (It's not as scary as it sounds)

Put your phone on vibrate or sound off, shut your door and most importantly close down extra windows on your computer. Believe me, if you have your emails open and you get one during the online talk, you will be distracted.

So why take that risk?

Reduce the distractions around you and focus on your online learning. It will almost certainly benefit you in the future and it's that long term focus you need to have.

I hope you found this useful.

Have a great day!

References:

vanDellen, M. R., Shah, J. Y., Leander, N. P., Delose, J. E., & Bornstein, J. X. (2015). In Good Company: Managing Interpersonal Resources That Support Self-Regulation. Personality and Social Psychology Bulletin, 41(6), 869–882. https://doi.org/10.1177/0146167215580778

https://www.psychologytoday.com/gb/articles/201509/distraction-101

PART TWO: EXAMS

# A STUDENT'S GUIDE TO UNIVERSITY AND LEARNING

HOW TO REMAIN CALM DURING A UNIVERSITY EXAM?

As psychology students it is fairly safe to say we have a good understanding of the importance of mental health, and why it is critical to look at.

That's why I'm opening this chapter and next section of the book by focusing on it specifically. Since it is so fundamental to your health, your exams and making sure you're okay which is the most important thing when you're at university.

<u>How To Remain Calm During A University Exam?</u>

It is very common to feel stressed out during an exam, students panic, convince themselves they'll fail and lots of negative things can happen during the exam. As well as this is what's missed a lot when people talk about exam stress, they talk about the stress before and after the exam. But never the exam itself. Therefore, in this blog post, I'll tell you how to remain calm during a university exam.

Believe In Yourself

A lot of exam stress comes from you not believing in yourself, you might believe you'll fail the exam, not achieve what you want and your degree might be devastated by the exam if you don't do well on it.

At first glance, this all sounds logical, it sounds normal to believe in these things.

However, you're forgetting a very important thing about exams. You are an amazing university student, you've studied hard for the exam, you've practised and you've made sure you are as prepared for this exam as possible.

You need to remember this.

You haven't been one of these students who's panicking because they didn't do any revision or practice for it. You're a student who has tried to make sure they'll do well in the exam.

So please, stop putting so much pressure on yourself and start believing in yourself. Because there's an extremely high chance you're going to do amazing. I remember times when I thought I wasn't going to do well in an exam to be surprised later on, that's happened lots of different times.

There's no reason it can't happen to you.

You've got this, you just need to believe it!

The World Won't End

Another major factor I've heard from other university students is they believe the world will end if they don't get a certain grade in the exam. Of course you want to do well during your exams but you might come across a question that triggers all your fears about doing well in the exam.

In all honesty, the world will not end if you don't get a certain grade. Life will continue and so will your degree, because I'll tell you now, it is extremely difficult to fail a university exam. Since a fail is 40%.

Therefore, I'm saying, yes do your hardest to get the best exam result you can. But don't stress out about it, your world will continue if you don't.

Also I should note from personal experience that external influence (parents, friends and more) can put pressure on you during an exam. Their expectations can pop up at the worse times, but they don't matter in an exam. This isn't their life, their exam, their degree.

Personally I would like to see some of my family members try and answer some of the questions I've had to do for my exams. They couldn't do them, I know that for sure.

All in all, when you're in an exam, no one else matters and your world will continue. Thus, just try your best and answer every single question.

<u>Do The Exam</u>

Building upon the last section, you just need to put away all of the critical voice and just do the exam. It's better you tried your hardest in the exam and get a bad mark, than not doing the exam because of fears and stress, and getting a bad mark.

In my opinion I would remember what I've said

in this blog post, your world will continue, what other people think doesn't matter and believe in yourself. Then just carry on with the exam.

I know it's hard sometimes but you aren't doing the exam for other people, you aren't doing it so you can compare with your friends. You're doing it because you want to develop your knowledge and get a grade for your future career.

But even then, it is just an exam at the end of the day. It isn't going to hurt you and as long as you've tried your best. Then that's all you can do.

Conclusion:

Overall, I hope you found this blog post useful and you now have some things to bear in mind and remember when you're next in an exam. I know it's difficult but we do need to get through the critical voice and do the exam.

I hope you found it useful and I wish you all the best of luck on your next exam!

HOW SHOULD STUDENTS PREPARE FOR EXAM SEASON?

Preparation in life really is everything and that is still extremely true for university and exams. If you aren't prepared for your exams, then guess what, you'll probably do bad or worse than if you were prepared.

But how do you prepare yourself?

That's the focus of this next chapter.

How Should University Students Prepare For Exam Season?

With the exam season only two or three months away, I cannot encourage you enough to start preparing yourself now. Therefore, when the exam season does start you are more prepared and it is a lot less likely that you'll get overwhelmed. So please expect plenty of useful tips in today's blog post.

How To Prepare For The Exam Season?

The simplest way to start preparing for the exam season is by starting to look at what exams you actually have. As well as sometimes you can be extremely smart about your exams, because sometimes you're able to minimize the number you have.

For example, as I write this post, I've just chosen by final year modules and thankfully there were more than enough interesting modules to choose that didn't have any exams. Of course, this might not be available to you, or you might do better in an exam compared to coursework. We are all different and you need to do what is right for you.

Therefore, you need to look at your exams so you know how many you need to prepare for, but you need to double check the details of the exams too. For example, during my second year, lots of my exams were different to each other. Some of them were open book, others were closed and the rest were multiple choice questions.

This sort of "deeper" understanding of your exams will really help you plan and prepare for them.

For instance, if you have five exams. Three of them were open book (meaning you can have a textbook open next to you) but the other two were closed book exams with two essay questions each. Then that is extremely important to factor in since you technically have more to revise in the essay exams compared to the open book ones. Considering in the essay exams you need to know all your citations and references off by heart, that is slightly less needed in the open book exams.

Anyway, all this will depend on your own exams and how they work. I do not envy law and accounting students. Their exams sound hard!

<u>Create A Revision Plan</u>

I know you've probably been told that millions of times and I know it can get extremely tiring but it is important. As well as when you factor in the importance of knowing your different exams then a revision plan can get very effective.

Therefore, all you need for that is create a few sessions in your busy university schedule that drops completely in the exam season to start revising your different modules. And to be honest, the reason this post is early and before the exam season is simple.

Start revising before the exam season!

That will give you plenty of time to see what you know, what you need to revise and improve on.

Then if you need to get the extra help then this buffer between you starting early and the exam season gives you the time to get it.

For example, let's say you gave yourself ten hours a week to study (do not take that as advice) and you have five exams to study for. Theoretically that means you have two hours a week for each exam, but you might not need that.

I know if I was doing this, I wouldn't need that long to study for a clinical psychology exam since I know it fairly well due to my podcast and other activities. But I know cognitive (mental processes) psychology a lot less well because it is a bit more complicated, so I might spend an hour on clinical psychology and three on cognitive.

That is why knowing your exams is so important, and this sort of flexibility needs to be put into your revision plan. As at the end of the day, you need to create a revision plan (and actually do it) that will help you as much as it can.

Then I recommend you find out what revision techniques work for you as well. There's no point in you using a technique because it is *"the right way to revise"* if it isn't working for you.

Conclusion:

This post really has scratched the surface of a very important topic that will be explored in future posts. But I really do recommend you start revising early, I know it doesn't sound fun but it is helpful, and I know whenever I have started something early I am really grateful I did that.

It definitely prevents all the stress of working right up to a deadline!

Therefore, start early, create a revision plan and revise effectively for you.

The exam season doesn't have to be scary, and those three things can definitely help you avoid the fear.

ONLINE EXAMS FOR UNIVERSITY STUDENTS: A STUDENT'S PRESPECTIVE

In case you do end up doing online exams, then I thought it might be helpful for you to understand how it feels, especially if you're experiencing this for the first time, so the focus of the next chapter is telling you my own experience of these types of exams. In an effort to relax and help you and hopefully reveal what they're actually like compared to all the myths.

Online Exams For University Students: A Student's Perspective

When I was asked to write this post, I was rather pleased actually. Since it isn't often I get to do a blog on purely my own experience, and I really want to stress to all of you university students that online exams aren't evil, more difficult than in-person exams nor something to be scared of. So by the end of this post, you should start feeling more confident about online exams and I'll share with you my own experience with them.

Of course everything in this post is just my own opinions and experiences, and things might be different for you. But this post is filled with great concepts and ideas that you can draw on.

What Did I Think of Online Exams Before I Took Them?

I won't lie to you.

When I first learnt that I was going to be doing my exams online for the foreseeable future in April 2020, I was concerned. I didn't know how they were going to work, if they would be fair and if I would do terrible at them.

I'm hardly the only person to feel like this, so if you're concerned about them. You aren't alone but you don't need to feel like this for a few different reasons. Some of which I'll discuss now.

If you're in your first year at university and you have online exams, in my experience you have it the easiest like I did. Since our first university exams are almost always multiple choice questions and we simply need to choose the right answer.

If these are your exams then you really don't have anything to worry about, because the online exam is identical to the real in-person exam. You simply click on the correct answer.

Personally, I was really glad to have my first year exams online, because they were easy to do and I managed to get them done very quickly. Of course,

NEVER rush exams and always check over your answers, but the nice thing about online exams is once you've done them. You can go.

And considering I had a forensic psychology exam on my birthday, I didn't want to do an exam for any longer than I had to.

However, I'm sure some of you are wondering about "proper" exams for second and third year students.

How Did I feel About my Second Year Exams Being Online?

This is where the student perspective comes in, because I would never say this section in public or in front of lecturers.

Since I was extremely pleased with my second year exams being online, because I am not the best academic writer. Give me a nonfiction or fiction book, a short story or a blog post, and I can write that easily enough. But give me an essay to write and I flaunter massively.

Thanks to the great people at my placement, I don't think that will be as much of the case next year, but during my second year I was very bad at academic writing. I knew the information like the back of my hands, but according to the university professors, I couldn't phrase the information in an academic manner to their liking.

Now I made that clear because I want other people who struggle with academic writing to know that things can improve (If you try to improve).

Anyway, online exams are great for people like me because of one very special reason.

That is the university knows people will cheat and some modules try to remedy the situation. It goes without saying but don't cheat in your exams, that will only hurt you in the long run. But most of my essay writing exams during my second year were changed from closed book to open book exams, meaning I could have textbooks and notes around me.

Now this is flat out ideal because my problem with university exams is each lecture can be broken down into tens of little subareas, each of which could be an essay question. Therefore, I find the idea of revising for essays to be extremely daunting and I have no idea how I will manage in my third year.

However, with online exams tending to be open book that solves that problem. Online exams in my experience allow you to have your textbooks and notes around you.

Personally I think that was a lifesaver during my second year, and this is what I mean when I say online exams aren't scary or evil things. If you understand how to approach them, they can actually be extremely positive things.

Still I need to add, always check your exams because some of them might still be closed book, and of course don't cheat. Cheating is never good and it will seriously harm you in the long term, and you really don't want to be kicked out of university for something as silly as cheating in an exam.

Conclusion:

Looking back at my online exam experience, I won't lie- it was great. It was great to have slightly different exams that positively affected me. I know lots of people do find academic writing difficult even if they know the information, since universities just expect you to know how to write academically.

But that's a different blog post.

So I want to finish up by saying that online exams… they aren't scary, concerning or something you need to get anxious about. Exams are important for sure, but online exams can be great things if you know how to approach them.

Never see anything at university as a chore or evil because that will only lead to you feeling sad, down and like university isn't fun. And you should never feel like that. So please, look at online exams as something interesting to experience and maybe even a slightly better alternative to the traditional in-person exams we all grew up doing.

BEING KIND TO YOURSELF DURING EXAM SEASON FOR UNIVERSITY STUDENTS

When it comes to university exams no one ever thinks of this critical topic that really helps your mental health.

Therefore, I highly recommend reading this chapter even if you are perfectly fine with exams, because ever if this chapter doesn't help you spefifically it might be invaluable to a friend or family member.

And I think everyone will find this presepctive very fresh, interesting and different.

Being Kind To Yourself During Exam Season For University Students

With the exam season coming ever closer, it is always a good idea to go over the basics. Like, the revision timetable, make sure you start revising early and revision techniques. That is all well and good but there is a critical factor that so many students miss out on and it can lead to devastating consequences. That is not relaxing and making time for yourself. So in this blog post, I'll explain why it's important, how to do and most importantly, how to find a balance.

Why Is Being Kind To Yourself During Exam Season Important?

For a lot of different people, regardless of how studious you are, this is a very difficult topic because of the whole academic environment. Since we are told when we are at university, we should be studying constantly and I think for every one hour of university teaching, you're meant to do five hours of independent learning.

I'm still can't (or refuse to) remember how many times I got told that during my first year.

However, the point is during our university life, we are told we are meant to do a lot of studying and revising and preparing for exams.

As a result, this leads to us to believe that we cannot afford to take any time off or do anything fun otherwise we risk our chances at a very good grade.

The reality?

To be honest, if you work really hard, at all hours of the day and you never have time for yourself. Then something very simple will happen to you. You burn out, become overwhelmed and you will just not want to study (or you at least won't retain the information you're trying to absorb. But that's a different blog post altogether).

Meaning you will theoretically be doing all the

right things by studying hard, but you'll burn out and you will forget the information you learn. Leading to bad grades.

The solution?

You simply need to be kind to yourself during exam season and make sure you have a balance between studying and having time for yourself.

<u>How Do You be Kind To Yourself?</u>

In my experience, there are four main ways for you to be kind to yourself for exams.

The first is very easy. You don't push yourself to the extreme. Now everyone has very different levels of comfort when it comes to studying. Some people can revise for half an hour at a time with a ten minute break then go back to it. Other people can revise for hours at a time without a break.

Personally and this is sort of degree-informed, I should recommend you do have regular breaks and maybe stick with half an hour to an hour revision sessions. But you need to do what works for you.

Secondly, it's important to make sure you work hard, but not to the extreme. It's good for everyone to push themselves slightly but only if that push benefits them. For example, if you believe you can only effectively revise three topics a day. Maybe try to revise a fourth, that way you get to revise more in the long term.

However, if you do that and you realise that fourth topic wasn't done as effectively as the first three. And it made you feel really tired, then maybe stick to your three topics a day. You just need to experiment and see what works for you.

As a saying goes in clinical psychology: *you are the expert in you*. So only you know what works for you and your revision, but be willing to try other things.

Revision Comparison:

Thirdly, and I was extremely confused when I first heard people do this, please do not compare yourself to other people. Of course, I know people compare themselves to others for things like bodies (don't do that), relationships and more. But I didn't know some people compare others for the amount of revision they do.

Now that is just… silly, and I must stress to you, please do not do that. Not only will that lead to a decrease in revision and an increase in burnout over the long term, but it'll just make you feel miserable. Why put yourself through that?

Therefore, if you feel yourself compare the amount of revision you do to someone else. Just stop. Focus on your own revision, do your best and make time for relaxing and you should be fine.

Actively Plan Your Relaxation Time

Finally (and this is the most important point), you need to actively plan your relaxation time and make sure you actually do things away from your revision area some days. Like, go out with friends and family, go to different places, go to the beach. Just go somewhere where you can unwind, relax and re-energised so you can come back to the textbooks and be ready to absorb more information for your exams.

Personally, during exam season, I make sure I go out with friends and family and I go out before exam season to different places. This allows me to be energised and ready for the exam season. For example, if this was my exam season this year, it would be good that I'm going up to London for a few days for a major international conference. This would allow me to study hard for a few days before I went, relax during the conference and then return re-energised afterwards.

Therefore, I doubt anyone of you go to conferences, but there are other parts of my example that you can take. Like going out with friends and family members.

Also, if you need something relaxing for a few hours, read a book, watch a film or do something else. Just make sure you do relax.

How To Find A Balance During Exam Season?

Bearing all of that in mind, you need to make sure you don't spend so much time relaxing that you don't get any studying done. It's a strange paradox. Leading someone (probably you or me) to ask the question of how do you find a balance?

And if you remember the last exam season post: *How Should University Students Prepare for Exam Season*, you should factor in relaxation time into your revision schedule. As well as this serves an extremely important for you. It makes sure the revision timetable is something that you stick to because instead of it being a tortuous, boring chore. It will be something you're more likely to enjoy because you know if you do X amount of studying, you get to do Y as a relaxation reward afterwards.

Overall, just try to strike a balance between studying and being kind to yourself. Maybe go for 50:50, 60:40 (studying: relaxing) or whatever helps you do the best you can possibly do.

Conclusion:

We've spoken about a lot of things in this blog post, but here are the highlights:

- Be kind to yourself to avoid burnout
- Factor in some relaxation time by going out and doing things you enjoy. These activities will help you feel re-energised.
- Strike a balance between enough study time so you get good grades, with enough relaxation time to avoid burnout.

I hope you learnt something!

HOW TO DEAL WITH STRESS AND ANXIETY WHEN WAITING FOR EXAM MARKS?

After you're done your exams and revision, there comes a time for some people where they are stuck waiting for their marks and they hate it. It can lead to stress and anxiety and this really hurts their mental health.

Hopefully, after reading this next chapter I can spare you some or if not all of this emotional pain.

We all hate waiting for the marks, but some people have other side effects. I really hope this helps.

Enjoy!

How To Deal With Stress and Anxiety When Waiting For Exam Marks?

After recently going through this myself, I understand why some students get stressed and anxious whilst they wait for their university marks. Personally, I had to wait to find out if I was going on my placement year and the uncertainty of my next university year was awful.

In this post, I'll explain some tips and tricks to help you deal with this stress and anxiety. Mainly we'll be focusing on the mental health side of this topic because this is what can harm you over time.

<u>Why Is Waiting for Exam Marks Stressful?</u>

I wanted to add this section because I really want you to know that you aren't the only university student feeling like this. We all get nervous, anxious and stressed out about our exams.

After an entire year of hard work, hard deadlines and almost impossible lectures, we need to know we've done well.

We need to know we've been successful.

Sadly, there's a large time delay between our exams and us getting our results. This can't be helped but it's still stressful.

<u>Enjoy The Time Delay</u>

My first big tip to you is reframe how you see this time delay between the exams and results. Don't see this as a scary time until you know your fate for the next university year.

See it as an amazing reward and three months off university for you to enjoy. This links to the other blogs on the website about Relaxation and enjoying yourself.

Therefore, I suggest you make the most of this time by going out with friends and family, doing what you love and having fun. Because I know from experience it isn't long until you're back at university again!

Your Feelings Are Temporary

I borrowed this tip from a podcast I'll link to down below and this is important. Due to your feelings of stress and anxiety are temporary. You aren't going to feel them forever.

As a result, you can bear this in mind, allow yourself to feel what you're feeling but know these feelings will go away.

Other Stress Reduction Tips:

I could easily talk about stress reduction for ages but we need to talk about the marks themselves.

The University Marks

With this being the source of a person's anxiety and stress, it's important to talk about them.

First and foremost, there are just marks. They are your results on a standardised test that show your knowledge at a point in time. They aren't the end of the world and if you're reading a blog like this then chances are, you've tried your best. That's all anyone can ask of you.

Expectations of Marks and Getting What You need

Leading me onto another point, please don't set your expectations too high. For example one of my university friends, he's extremely smart and he rightfully sets his expectations high. But he was disappointed with a 75 before because he expected an 80 something.

At the end of the day, that result is still a very good first but he got disappointed because his expectations were off.

In terms of you, I want to say adjust your expectations accordingly to protect yourself from disappointment. For example, we know the standard is a 2:1 at university which is at least a 60. As well as with a 2:1 you can get into graduate programmes (hopefully), do years in industry and more.

Therefore, if you're stressing out that you need a first or a score of 70. Ask yourself why? Are you setting expectations higher than needed?

Of course, try to get a first (if you want) but it's okay if you only get a 60.

Conclusion:

Overall, the point of this blog post is to emphasise I know waiting for university marks is horrific. But you need to relax and focus on the free time you now have.

However, if your marks are concerning you then make sure you understand you only need to get what you need for your next stage of university.

I know this is a very difficult topic but I hope you found it useful.

Have a great day!

PART THREE: COURSEWORK TIPS

COURSEWORK TIME MANAGEMENT

Coursework.

There is something that we all love and hate about it. Personally, I love how I have more time to prepare and I can use tons of textbooks for citations with coursework, but it is still something that can be very difficult at times.

However, time management is a critical aspect to be successful when it comes to coursework, so definitely read this next chapter.

Coursework Time Management For University Students

When it comes to university there are lots of tasks you need to keep track of and manage. For example, a typical university week could involve going to five lectures, doing the 5 lots of reading, maybe a bit of extra research and a seminar or two. This is before we consider the relaxing and spending time with friends that are critical for maintaining your mental health.

Therefore, from that quick paragraph we know there is a lot to do at university, but can this get any busier?

Yes!

Add to that typical week, the researching and writing of a piece of coursework then you could have a bit of a time management problem.

Thankfully in today's post I'm going to tell you three tips to help you!

(And too many professionals have called me the Master of Time Management so I think you're in good hands)

<u>Prioritise and Breaking Down Tasks:</u>

I know this sounds so simple, so easy and it is often the easy things we don't think will work. But I promise you if you start to Prioritize your workload things will get so much easier. As prioritising allows you to see what tasks are actually important and when you should do them.

For example, if you're module sets you to write a five thousand word essay in three weeks, in addition to all the reading and lectures you normally have. At first this sounds awful and like the worse thing imaginable, but you need to take a step back and break the task down.

Since an essay can easily be broken down into a few stages: researching, writing the introduction, three/ four main body paragraphs, the critical thinking sections and the conclusion. Then the formatting, proofreading and submitting.

Again, ten things sounds awful.

However, you need to remember that some of these take less time than others, and your prioritising will be handy.

For example, you have three weeks to write the essay. Thus, you could prioritise your readings for that week's lecture first, then you could spend the rest of the week researching your essay. Meaning that's done by Friday or Sunday night.

The next week, you could again prioritise the readings and seminar prep for that week. Giving you the rest of the week to write the introduction, main body and critical thinking sections.

In the last week, you might want to switch the priorities around so you finish writing the essay, do the proofreading, formatting and submit it before you do that week's reading.

In all honesty, you need to decide what works best for you and how you work. The example above was only a quick example of how you could potentially break down a task into more manageable chunks. Then prioritising your existing workload with your coursework.

Overall, I cannot stress enough that if you break down the sections of what your coursework contains then it does seem a lot more manageable and easier to do. Since you can do one section at a time and feel like you're making progress towards completing an amazing piece of coursework.

Scheduling:

Personally, this is my favourite way and this is how I'm able to do so much in the different areas of my life. Due to I loosely schedule everything in a balanced way that allows me to do lots of things.

For example, when I had a psychology essay to write, I would schedule Monday and Tuesday to be time where I focused on that week's lectures and readings, as well as since this is was all online all the lectures were pre-recorded.

Then for the rest of the week, I could easily work on my essay but I scheduled it in a sustainable way. For example, after breakfast, I would go on the bike, do some exercise as this helps to maintain mental health. Then I would shower and everything before spending an hour on my essay. Afterwards I would have a break (have a KitKat!) where I would talk to parents and do socially based things before having another hour on my essay. I would repeat this another two times.

Resulting in me having four hours of focused essay time.

However, the reason why scheduling is so important to me is because scheduling allowed me to still work on my essay for four hours but it allowed me to easily fit in other things. Like, exercise, social activities, breaks and more. And I'll tell you something, I didn't get stressed once about my essay.

Conclusion:

The entire point of this post wasn't too often

official advice or tips. This was an awareness post to get you thinking about what you might want to do and the tricks to use to try and make your life easier.

Of course, my scheduling and priorities might not work for you. but something else might, so try them, think about what works for you and your life.

Essays don't have to be hard or traumatic, so please don't feel like they have to be. Learn habits, learn skills, just learn ways to make coursework less stressful for you, and you should be fine.

University can be a great time in your life, don't let coursework bog you down!

HOW TO PREPARE FOR GROUP PROJECTS AT UNIVERSITY?

As you'll see in this chapter I hate group projects and that is exactly who this chapter is designed for.

If you hate group projects then you must read this next chapter as it will definitely help you to overcome at least some of your concerns and fears about this awful area of university coursework.

How To Prepare Yourself For Group Projects At University?

Even that title must have struck fear in the hearts of many students, I have heard from countless numbers of students how much they don't like the idea of group projects. I was no exception, so the purpose of today's post is to help show you why they aren't the stressful, evil, horrible assessment that everyone fears them to be.

Why Do Students Hate Group Projects?

There never is one answer to these sorts of things but there are a range of themes that pop up when you ask students. The most prevalent theme is some version of when you're working by yourself, if you screw up then it is your fault. But when you're in a group then other people could cause your mark to fall and that stress or concern never feels good.

In addition, all these concerns tend to come from past experiences, because we can all remember times in groups when people haven't pulled their weight and they've left it to the rest of the group to sort out.

This has been my own experience more times than I care to admit because when I'm in a group most of the time, it has been left to me to sort out everything. Meaning because of all these experiences, I am not the biggest fan of group work, but I have changed my mindset in recent years on them.

And that's the key theme I'll be explaining in this blog post. When you change your mindset and perception of group work it can be more rewarding.

How To Prepare Yourself For Group Projects?
Communicate

We all know communication is key to group work and it can help us to sort out problems, but this is hard. It is really hard to have good communication in groups filled with people we don't know or have a good relationship with. Meaning most of the time we simply put up with the problems and hope that the group work will end sooner rather than later.

Additionally, this is very much a cultural thing. I know that in some cultures they aren't as preoccupied with avoiding conflict and voicing concerns than the

English. But when it actually comes to enjoying, benefiting and learning from group work, we all need to have good communication.

As well as when you voice your concerns about something isn't working, you think someone might be doing something wrong amongst other things. It is how you say it that can make a real difference.

For example, if someone thought you were doing something wrong and they moaned at you. You aren't going to like that and you probably won't respond or listen to the person. But if they said they liked your work but you might want to try this (insert whatever is appropriate here), then you are more likely to listen.

All in all, when in a group, communicate effectively. Not only will this help you to sort out any problems you have and this will make the whole experience more pleasant for everyone. But you might discover something that hadn't thought of before because someone might mention something interesting.

Take Advantage

When it comes to group work, there are lots of potential benefits and things to take advantage of.

Now I want to do this section to highlight how group work isn't bad and it does have a lot of great benefits. If only you are open to them and want to take advantage of the benefits.

For example, group work allows you to access the knowledge of over people, and if you're struggling with a particular skill then ask your group. They may be able to help you, and the same goes for if you don't understand a particular topic.

And I should admit that I am terrible for this, because I tend to avoid all of this. But please don't be like me, swallow your pride and ask for help. It won't make you look bad in front of your peers, it will allow you to improve, learn and hopefully get a better mark, be it now or in the future.

<u>Relax</u>

In an earlier section, I explained that lots of students don't like group work because of the stress it causes them, so this is something we need to address.

Just relax.

It's honestly great that you're concerned about your grades because it means you want your degree bad enough to care about it. But getting stressed out about group work isn't going to help you.

Group work is out of your control to some extent because the other group members will influence the work, but this isn't always a bad thing. Sometimes the other members will have great ideas and can write in such an academic way that it increases your marks.

Also group work can be a good break or palate cleanser from the normal solo assignments, so relax and try and enjoy them. Or at least don't get stressed out by them.

Looking at my own experience my first group project at university, I got extremely stressed out and it wasn't a good time for me. But looking back, I know now I should have relaxed more and calmed down.

Because the thing is, group works are never going to decide your fate at university. The solo assignments always have more bearing on your grades, so focus on them, try your best at group work and make sure you can be proud of what you contributed. But don't stress yourself out to the point you get ill about them.

Group projects aren't worth that level of stress, and I never want you to become ill.

<u>Final Major Benefit and Conclusion:</u>

Additionally, another major benefit of group work is it does give you skills to use in later life. Since we all need to know how to work with a wide range of people and that is what you get at university. You get so many amazing, interesting people from a wide range of backgrounds with their own experiences, knowledge and more.

Therefore, I cannot encourage you enough to take advantage of that. Talk to them, learn from their experiences and deepen your knowledge about how others live.

At the end of the day, group work isn't meant to be awful, hard or difficult. It is all part of the university learning experience and it can be great fun. If that's your mindset.

I've had some of my best conversations and realisations whilst talking to other people during group work and learning about their very different life to my own.

At worse, you'll be surprised about the experiences of some people.

At best, group work will allow you to deepen your understanding towards different people, you'll understand their struggles, their interests and why they are how they are. All these are amazing skills for now and in the future, so take advantage and see what you discover.

HOW TO PREPARE FOR PRESENTATIONS AT UNIVERSITY?

Again this is another area of coursework that I personally hate and I know I am far from alone in this area. Therefore, if you have any trouble about presentations then this is a very useful chapter for you as we discuss a lot of ways to help you prepare for rather terrifying form of assessment.

<u>How to Prepare For Presentations At University?</u>

The vast majority of degrees at university will involve some sort of presentation at some point during your degree. For the vast majority of students, this is something they hate because they are concerned about what would happen, them making a mistake and they could get a low grade. I understand all of this, so in today's post I'm going to be explaining how to prepare yourself and how to think about presentations.

However, before we talk about how to prepare for presentations, I want to remind you that there are benefits to doing them. As presenting information and getting comfortable with presenting can be a valuable skill in the job market, and it can help your confidence improve. Therefore, I know presentations can be horrible and scary, but they are still great practice for the real world.

<u>Be Prepared:</u>

Of course being prepared for a presentation is critical, but most students just prepare themselves in terms of their slides and the material. This is great and it will definitely help you, but this only goes so far.

As well as I highly recommend you at least try what one of my friends did in my first year, because she had a presentation and the night before, she practised in front of us.

I fully admit this is terrifying at first thought, but it is actually great practice for the real thing. For the main reason that you could have extra nerves about presenting in front of friends, family and whoever else you present in front of that you know. Since you will have to see these people again, you know if you mess up they will remember.

But this is actually a good thing.

Since if you can master presenting in front of these people then presenting in front of effectively strangers should be easy, or at least a lot easier.

Additionally, in terms of the planning and preparing yourself, you can always trust Active Class to help you. As it allows you to see your schedule and timetable so you can plan effectively for your preparation time.

Finally, sometimes you might have to do group presentations, now I luckily have only had to do these types of presentations. I honestly don't think I could handle a solo presentation very well but that's what I want to highlight. When you're in a group, it is easier because the focus isn't on you, it's on you and everyone else. Meaning if you make a mistake, no one will remember.

All in all preparation is key and don't take it for granted.

It's Okay To Make Mistakes:

Leading us onto my next point, I have never ever seen a presentation without a mistake. Just think back to our lectures, seminars, workshops, etc. our lecturers do make mistakes. But do we criticise them and think badly of them?

No.

We all know that mistakes are part of life and everyone makes them, so if you make a few it's okay. It is natural for you to forget something, stumble over your words or have to check the slides.

It's okay.

Of course, it is far better if you make it look natural and you can recover from your mistake without anyone noticing. For example, if you've forgotten what to say next, then you could talk a bit more about the topic whilst you check the slide again.

Overall, if you make a mistake, no one is going to moan, criticise or yell at you. We all know mistakes happen and as the old adage goes, it's all in the recovery.

One mistake doesn't defy a presentation.

<u>It Isn't Everything</u>

Even if you aren't the worse, the best or you're in the middle, it isn't everything. Your university grades won't be dependent on a single presentation and you will hardly be the only person who feels anxious. Meaning if you hate presentations and are fundamentally not good at them. Of course, keep learning, keep developing and keep trying to improve because you never know, one day you might become a great speaker.

But if you don't and you mess up on a presentation, it isn't the end of the world, and that is what students need to remember. There will always be other assignments, essays and assessments to increase your marks on.

No one is perfect at everything (I'm certainly not) so please stop holding yourself to such high standards. It's okay not to be good at presentations as long as you try.

I'm going to leave you at the end of this post by saying, presentations are the bane of many people's lives. But they don't have to be, you can practice, improve and enjoy them. Yet you have to want to enjoy them as with everything at university, everything needs to have a mindset of play and curiosity. And presentations are no exception.

No matter how scary they may seem.

RADICAL NEW IDEA TO IMPROVE ACADEMIC WRITING

To wrap up this section on coursework tips, I thought I would throw in this rather abstract or strange blog post I wrote once.

Of course I don't expect any of you to do it, but I have dapbled in this technique since I wrote this post and it is useful.

So skip, read or read it and maybe try it out. It's your choice but this might be very useful to some people.

Radical New Idea To Improve Academic Writing For University Students

This is probably one of my most abstract posts for this blog but I truly do believe in the idea. Since at university, we all want to improve our academic writing and this only becomes more true for people who don't have the natural talent for academic writing. I certainly don't have a talent for it, but people can improve in their writing.

As well as for a note of comfort to people who struggle with academic writing, I was talking to my brilliant supervisor the other day and he said that he was still learning about academic writing. Therefore, no one is a master of this topic, all we can do is learn and improve.

Moreover, what really got me thinking about my radical idea was when my placement supervisor mentioned that he used to know someone that had such a way with words that he could always sell papers to the best journals (We all want that!). Leading me to remember a concept from fiction writing and how there are levels of skill to writing.

Which brings me onto my main point.

<u>My Radical Idea:</u>

Now I should probably mention that I haven't tried out this idea in terms of academic writing but I have in fiction writing, and this works. This really, really works and because I know it works and I've improved because of it. I have no problem busting a few myths here.

As a result in professional fiction writing, no one tells you that all the long term professionals type in the openings, cliffhangers and more of other authors' work. They do this to train themselves and see what the author did so when they're writing next, their creative voice can use what it's learnt and write better stories. I know it sounds strange but this technique does work (and I shortened the actual explanation).

Anyway, I truly believe this can be applied to

academic writing because by typing in paragraphs of an academic paper you can train yourself to type the types of words they use, the sentence lengths and you can also learn why the author of the paper uses certain words. As you'll be typing along, you'll go to write a particular word because it's what you would say, only to find out the author used another word.

Then after you're finished typing out the paragraphs, you look and dive down into what you've typed. Since you'll be able to understand the word choices and you might discover things that you missed whilst you were typing.

All in all I know this sounds strange and very boring. But as I mentioned before on this blog, university and being a successful student is about developing a learning mindset, and this is just another step in learning.

In addition, I should add in terms of fiction, I never wanted to do this studying and typing in other authors' work. But once I started, I never ever looked back because now I know it works and it has really helped me improve as a writer.

Therefore, I fully intend to do this in my final year of university and hopefully this will help improve my essays, reports and dissertation.

Conclusion:

To wrap up today's blog post, I just wanted to say that even if you don't decide to do this radical idea (I know no one will), I wanted to show you that academic writing and improving in this particular type is possible but it requires learning. Whether you do this method, you read more academic papers or do something else entirely. You must always be learning if you wish to improve your writing skills, regardless of the type of writing you're doing.

As well as I wanted to show you that learning never ends in academic (or any) writing because you will never be the best. But that's what makes it interesting and fun, so please don't see academic writing as a boring skill that's a chore. See it as something new to learn and discover as you develop your new skills.

Because that's how you improve, and get better marks at university.

PART FOUR: GENERAL SOCIAL TIPS FOR UNIVERSITY STUDENTS

A STUDENT'S GUIDE TO UNIVERSITY AND LEARNING

FINDING YOUR PEOPLE AT UNIVERSITY

To break up all this university and learning content, I wanted to spend the next section of the book focusing on the all important social side of university. Since university can be an extremely social and good time of your life if you know how to make friends and find new people.

In this chapter, I'm going to help you find your people at university and why this is so important.

Enjoy!

<u>Finding Your People At University</u>

This is probably one of the only blog posts I have ever resisted writing because this isn't my expert area. But I guess that means I am a good person to write it in the end. Therefore, in today's blog post I'll be giving you a few tips about how to find your people at university.

Note: as I am a UK student, there will be some things that are specific to UK universities, but the vast majority of points are universal.

Talk To People In Your Lectures and Be Proactive

This is an easy and a difficult tip to start off with because we all know we need to talk to others. We know we need to be social, talkative and be proactive if we want to find new people in any environment.

But this is scary.

I will fully admit I find this sort of thing difficult. I am not a massive fan of talking to new people in large groups amongst other things.

Yet I do encourage you to do it. I recommend you talk to new people, socialise, see where conversations take you. You might end up meeting someone really interesting, a person similar to yourself and hopefully a life long friend.

None of it is possible unless you take the first step and start talking to people.

Also I need to mention that everyone is in the same boat. Everyone in your lectures and seminars will be nervous, scared and anxious about meeting new people. There is nothing new here, so be kind to yourself and take the first step to talk to someone.

In addition, there is a great easy fact here that might help you. Giving you the world's easiest ice breaker. You are all there to study the same thing. Everyone in my lectures and seminars is there to study psychology, so something I got to remember for my final year is to use the very easy ice break of "what made you want to study psychology?" or some version of that.

Instant ice breaker and conversation starter.

I think most of this idea about finding your people is down to all of us to stop being nervous about meeting new people and taking that first step.

Join Societies

This is the UK specific thing I mentioned earlier, but for the international audience, UK universities have these large social clubs that are formed around a particular activity called Societies. These I cannot stress enough are great ways to meet people.

For example, in my first year of university, I was a member of the Baking Society and this was a brilliant way to meet other people who enjoyed baking and did other degrees. Meaning I could hear their experiences, get to know them and get to learn from them. It was a great few hours every week where I got to hang out with people like me.

Additionally, the great thing about societies is most universities have tons of them centred around any activity you can imagine. So I would recommend you check out your university's website to see what they offer, and if there are any that interest you, sign up and go to them. You could have a LOT of fun.

One of my friends in first year did the Quidditch society!

(And yes, that is the sport from Harry Potter)

Lastly, there are always academic societies available to students so this gives you another opportunity to mix with others students. Some of which will be from later stages at university so you can hear their experiences. That I do recommend you do.

Don't Stress Out

As I preluded to in the first section, we all get stressed out or concerned about making new friends, meeting and mixing with new people. But please try not to get stressed out. It isn't healthy and it could only make your concern worse.

I would just relax, just do what I'm mentioned and remember something else.

I first heard this in my second year from my Student Ambassador Mentor and she mentioned the very true fact that we will meet new people every term. Due to every term we will have new modules with different students and we will have to mix with them again.

Meaning there is never a lack of opportunity to meet new people.

The only thing there is a lack of interest in taking the opportunity.

And I know, I really know this is scary and lots of people don't want to take that first step. But I highly recommend you do because you never know where that first step could take you. A person to talk to, a friend for the rest of university or a true lifelong friend.

You will never know unless you take that first step.

WHY IS UNIVERSITY AN INTERESTING TIME FOR LGBT+ STUDENTS?

As you'll quickly see in this chapter, this was a very interesting post for me to write both personally and professionally.

Therefore, all I can say in this short introduction to the chapter is if you're LGBT+ definitely read it because this is very, very useful and insightful.

If you aren't, I would still highly recommend reading it because it's a short chapter (compared to academic textbooks) and it gives you a chance to see university and life from a different perspective.

As well as as psychology student getting to experience life from a different perspective is honestly one of the most valuable tools around.

Why Is University An Interesting Time For LGBT+ Students?

Given how this post should go out sometime in June, which is Pride month, and the recent coming out of UK Football Jake Daniels, I thought it would be interesting to write up a post on the topic. Now I say interesting for three main reasons. Firstly, any LGBT+ students should find this post useful for them experiencing university. Secondly, heterosexual students should find this post interesting as it actually outlines some of the differences between university experiences. But it should also be interesting for me because I have never ever spoken about being gay publicly in any way, shape or form due to personal reasons. So this first post should be very interesting indeed.

Note: of course this is just based on my own personal experiences with general lessons that can be applied to different people. But your experience will be different to mine. As well as for the sake of case and because writing out LGBT+ each time will disrupt the flow of the post, I'll refer to everyone in the group as *gay* throughout the post. I apologise in advance if this causes offence.

Why Is University An Interesting Time For Gay Students?

One of the reasons why I think this post is important for both those coming to university and are already there is because the things discussed in the post can be done at any time, as you'll see later on.

However, the reason why university is an interesting time for gay students is because there are opportunities. Since if you come from a background that doesn't allow gay students to explore themselves, get to know this part of them and mix with other gay people. Then university can be great for providing you an opportunity to explore this area of yourself.

Then even if you come from somewhere that freely allows you to mix and explore yourself, coming to university can give you even more opportunities.

As a result, as far as I know most universities (at least in the UK) have some sort of LGBT+ society (social club) or something that allows different people to mix, get to know each other and probably get introduced to the gay community.

Personally, I do wish that I had actually done this in my first year of university. Since I remember during Freshers' Week at my university there was a coffee morning for LGBT+ people. Looking back I wish I would have gone, met up and talked to them, but for personal reasons I didn't feel like I could have done that.

Then again, now I'm in a position in my personal life where I can do that, I am really considering joining in in these events when I return to university for my final year.

Overall, when it comes to university, regardless of the positivity of your gay background, can provide you with some great opportunities to meet, mix with and explore the gay community and the part of yourself you might never have been able to experience before.

And something I need to keep reminding myself of when it comes to wider society's attitudes towards gay people. As universities are filled with young adults, for the most part, they tend to be much more relaxed and basically don't care if you're gay. If you come from even a slightly negative background, that can take some time to get used to.

Support and Independence:

Another reason why university can be an interesting time for gay students is because there is a lot of support at universities. Which leads on slightly from the paragraph above, because the vast majority of students are fine with gay people. I've heard and seen that people are very supportive if there is a problem.

Again, if you haven't been in an environment where you could openly talk about being gay, the problems you face and the like. University can be a very strange place in that sense.

As well as it technically goes without saying, but if you aren't use to it then it is new to you, if you have a problem then there are other gay people at university that you can talk to. For example, if you have a problem about homophobic family members and friends, you aren't sure how to "come out" amongst other things. You can most probably find other gay people at university to talk to. You would probably have to start off with the LGBT+ society then go from there.

Even though I will admit I am looking forward to the day where "coming out" isn't needed anymore. I look forward to the day where it's a case of "I'm gay," then the person you're telling basically looks like that isn't new at all anymore.

Anyway, the independence of university can be a great boon for gay students in my opinion. Since if you live in a slightly anti-gay environment, it really does restrict what you are willing to do. For example, you cannot necessarily date, you cannot do to LGBT+-themed events and the rest. But if you do live away from home (which is not right for everyone I will remind you) then the independence can be good for you.

Again, I do personally wish I would have used this freedom in my first year of university. I do wish that I went to some events, meet-ups and engaged more with that part of myself. Maybe I will do that more in my final year, maybe not, but the independence university gives you can be useful.

My Point and Conclusion

As when I start writing most of these blog posts, I don't know where I'm going with it. I didn't even have a title when I started this one, because writing like this is so new to me. I simply didn't know what to write, but after the past 900 words, I think my point is very clear. But I have to admit it has felt good to talk about this stuff so openly, so thank you readers for letting me do it.

If you're an LGBT+ student, whether you're thinking of going to or are currently at university, then university can provide a lot of great opportunities to explore different aspects of yourself. This is great for people with completely supportive families, and it's even greater for people who don't necessarily have the wholehearted support of their entire families.

All I would say is, be open to the opportunities and embrace them as they come along as long as you are comfortable with them. Exploring your gay side (couldn't think of a better term) doesn't have to be a sprint. It's a marathon, so start slowly, have fun and enjoy your time at university.

And that goes for everyone!

FINDING YOUR PASSION AGAIN FOR UNIVERSITY STUDENTS

Because this chapter really does stand alone without me needing to add anything else to it, I just want to say READ IT!

Due to there will sadly be a time at university where you do struggle to find your passion for psychology (or whatever degree you do) and this chapter will come in very hand.

So please, don't skip this chapter.

<u>Finding Your Passion Again For University Students</u>

There will always be a time, or times, at university that will cause you to question why you are there, why did you pick your course and many more questions of self-doubt. Also during these difficult times, you will lose your passion for your degree topic and this can only add to your self-doubt and feelings of discontent. Therefore, in today's blog post, I'm going to explain how you can find your passion again as this will give you the drive to continue with your studies.

Why Does Passion Go For Students?

Believe me when I say I can talk from personal experience about losing your passion for your degree. There have been a good number of times where I have lost my passion, not for psychology but the whole university learning thing and all those assignments that come from university.

However, I am still here, I'm learning and looking forward to the rest of my university life, including continuing to learn more about my degree topic.

Yet there are lots of different reasons why people lose their passions. It could be because it wasn't what they thought it was, the degree is hard, they don't do well at assignments, no matter how hard they try amongst others.

But the most important thing to do when you have lost your passion, is to get back up and find it.

Hence the focus of today's post.

How To Find Your Passion Again?

Focus On Your Why

We all go to university for different reasons, and these are always really interesting to hear, but they are critical to remember when we lose our passion. Since these whys can remind us why you love your degree, why we chose it and what we want to achieve. All these things can help us to find our passion once more and carry on with our degrees.

For example, you might have chosen Law because you wanted to become a lawyer and work in

Company Law (The world's most random example, I know) because you wanted to help companies deliver their vision to the world.

But you're half way through your degree and you aren't doing as well as you wanted. Leading you to feel down and like you're wasting your time.

However, by remembering why you choose law. You should find you smile as you remember how badly you wanted to help these companies and this gives you the drive and passion to continue.

Therefore, whilst I admit that was a weird example (I'm extremely surprised I came up with it), I hope you can see that by remembering why you choose to do your degree in the first place, it can help you in the tough times.

Also even if you don't know a good reason why you went to university, try to find one, write it down and keep it somewhere safe. You never know when you might need it.

Focus On Your Reasons For The Topic

This next point is slightly different to the one above because that point focused on why did you go to university. This point focuses on why you choose what you did. For instance, I chose psychology because I find it really interesting, the jobs pay well and I was passionate about the topic. But I went to university because you can't get a job in psychology without a number of degrees.

Your reasons will probably be different.

However, I encourage you to think about why

you picked your degree subject and write them down so you can remember them in the bad times.

For example, if you're a Business student who chose business because you're passionate about business, how it works and you want to become a major business owner in the future. Then write down these reasons. If you ever get stuck or are feeling down during your degree, remind yourself of these reasons and your passion should return.

Don't Focus On The Future

Personally whenever I lose my passion it tends to be because I haven't done as well as I wanted to in an assessment. Then I started to notice that other people were having similar issues and the real problem all comes down to we are focusing too much on the future.

Now I admit I am a long term thinker, I can plan out years ahead, but this can and does come back to bite me when I do assessments. Since if I don't do well in assignments then I start to grow concerned about the future and the things I want to do in the long term.

I know I'm not alone.

Therefore, when you find yourself in doubt and your passion is lost, don't focus on the future. Focus on the now and what you can do to improve your situation and find your passion again.

For example, you could research and learn more so in the next assessment piece you could do better. Then return to your whys as well.

Conclusion:

I want to finish by saying that university, learning and everything else it involves is great. Sure it is difficult, annoying and disappointing sometimes, but more often than not university is a great place to be.

However, the times when you don't want to be there, just remember your whys, focus on what's important and don't focus on the future.

And hopefully you'll be fine.

PART FIVE: THE CHRISTMAS BREAK

HOW TO PREPARE FOR THE FINAL WEEK BEFORE CHRISTMAS AT UNIVERSITY?

As I haven't written the introduction to the book yet, I don't actually know if you know that I wrote the blog post these chapters are based on for the e-learning platform Active Class.

Therefore, for the Christmas break at university 2021, they asked me to write a series of blog posts for students so they could use the break effectively.

After reading this next section of the book, you'll definitely know that I prefer to have fun over Christmas, but there are a lot of other things you could do as well as have fun.

This is definitely an eye-opening and interesting section that no one really talks about.

<u>How To Prepare For The Final Week Before Christmas At University?</u>

The final week before Christmas at university is a strange time for all of us. It's an exciting time because we get to get home, be with our families or do whatever you have planned for the month off. Yet it's a strange time as well because as far as the university is concerned, it's just another week.

The only difference is there tends to be a lot of deadlines (and even exams!) during the last week, and sometimes there are my most unfavourited thing ever- group presentations! I hate them with a passion but that's not the purpose of this blog post.

Therefore, today's blog post is going to tell you how to prepare for the final week of university so you enjoy it, not get stressed and leave university happy, not grumpy.

Why Is The Last Week Filled With Deadlines?

I think it's good to be aware of why the deadlines are (admittedly) at a horrible time in the term because I remember seeing students always getting stressed and turn grumpy in the final week all because of these deadlines. Leading some students to ask why the lecturers were so horrible to set the deadlines for when they had.

Therefore, in case you're wondering the same thing, the reason is simple. It's all because during the term lecturers have to do lectures, planning and any other responsibilities that they have to do. As well as trying to grade hundreds of papers or whatever other type of assessment they had to mark on top of that is next to impossible.

Also the grades have to be moderated and everything else that goes into marking and quality assurance.

Meaning this is far, far, far easier to do over a long break like the Christmas break and the Easter break so that's why they tend to set the deadlines for then.

All in all, it isn't the lecturers trying to be mean when they set the deadlines, it's them trying to do their jobs to the best they can.

How To Prepare For The Final Week Of University?

Now that I've laid down the context, we can start to think about how can we prepare ourselves for this final week.

Plan Ahead

This definitely has been my saving grace during university and it's been a common theme during the blog posts. As when you know you'll have several deadlines coming up, then I highly recommend you plan out your time so you can use it effectively and don't get overwhelmed.

For example, let's say you have two exams and an essay due in the final week, which is six weeks away.

The first thing I would think about is, can I get the essay done now? That way it's finished and I can forget about it.

In my experience, most of the time you will be able to complete the essay a few weeks before the deadline if you've already been taught the topic and you chip away at it.

Even if you only chip away at it for a week or two, you'll be surprised how much you can get done over that time. This is a great trick for students that are too busy with other things, like readings, lectures and more.

In terms of the exams, what I use to do was starting from around 4 weeks away I would do a little revision each day so it didn't take up too much of my time, but it added up over time. For example, if an exam covered 14 different topics then I could easily do a topic a day for a month and cover each topic twice.

At the end of the day, you need to decide what works for you but I hope you can see the possible value of planning ahead and chipping away at tasks.

Make Sure You Go To Your lectures:

I wanted to break up the tips a little bit here because I know some of you reading this will not want to go to your lectures on the final week. I cannot blame you. I knew tons of people didn't go to some lectures on the final week because they wanted to go home and be with their family earlier.

Now I really can relate to this because I remember in my first year at university, I had some awful lectures on the final week that I could easily not go to. But I went and I made sure I leant about the topic, because I knew it would help in the future. As well as there is an extremely high chance you will be tested on the things you learnt in the last week of term, so do you really want to miss those possible marks?

Personally, I would recommend you go to the

lecture, learn some things and not take a possible risk in the future. And anyway, it's only a few hours of your life and then you'll get to see your loved ones for an entire month afterwards.

It doesn't seem that unfair to me.

Keep Your Drive

My final tip for you during the final week is keep your drive, passion and focus up.

I know during the last week, you're done, fed up and you just want to go home or wherever you're going. You've done university for an entire term and you just want a little break. Meaning your focus, drive and passion nose dives.

I've been there. I agree with you. But don't.

I really do encourage you to keep up your passion and drive during this week, and definitely find out ways to keep this up. Due to you're going to need the drive and focus when you quickly finish up the week's reading, assignments and doing the exams.

Believe me, you don't want to have no drive or focus during an exam!

All in all, focus on the fact that you only have one week left before the break. Give yourself one more week of drive, passion and focus and you'll almost certainly be thanking yourself in the future. As that drive will help in any exams, lectures and assignments you have that week.

The Best Thing

To wrap up this post I want to end on a very light note and I love this point.

Therefore, as this is university and NOT school, most universities don't end on Fridays so you'll probably have a shorter week anyway. I remember in my first year I had a full week because I had a forensic psychology lecture from 4 til 6 on the Friday (yes I wasn't happy) but my second year I was finished on the Tuesday.

So if you leave this blog post with anything, let it be that the final week isn't your enemy. It's an important week that can be a lot of fun and interesting, so look forward to the end and the Christmas break, but plan ahead, turn up to your lectures and keep your drive up and you should be fine.

Regardless of whether you celebrate Christmas or not, I wish you a great final week and a brilliant Christmas break.

WHAT TO DO OVER THE CHRISTMAS UNIVERSITY BREAK?

Continuing with our look at the university Christmas break, our next area of focus is the actual break itself and what you could be doing over it, in addition to relaxing and having fun, that might help your studies.

<u>What To Do Over The Christmas University Break?</u>

Whilst the answer will definitely depend on you as a person, this is a great topic to talk about because the Christmas break is a chance for university students to have four weeks off. But it is very rare for students to actually have that chance, leading us to the question of what to do over the Christmas university break?

In this blog post, I'll give a few ideas to inspire you if you want to do something productive during your break, whilst having a good amount of time to relax too.

Leading us onto our first one.

Relax: Yourself and See Friends and Family

I know this isn't anything new but I wanted to mention it because the Christmas break is a brilliant time to relax, catch up with people and see your friends and family again. This isn't just critical for your mental health and wellbeing, but it's critical for the sake of your relationships too. As during the past four months during the university term, I completely understand if you haven't seen certain family members or friends.

For example, I have a few university friends so they're busy during the term so I see them in the breaks. The same goes for family because they work, I'm busy with university so I see them in the breaks to make sure I still keep in contact with them and keep relationships alive.

You need to do the same.

Because seeing your friends and family will make you feel better and have other benefits for your mental health and wellbeing. As well as after a potentially stressful time during the university term, you need a break, and seeing friends and family is the perfect way to take a break.

Also I will fully admit it is really nice to see people outside of the university bubble.

Nonetheless, something that almost always gets overlooked in these sorts of posts is the importance of you taking time for yourself. I know you might not see spending some alone time as important but you need to do what you want to do for fun as a way to relax.

For instance, during the university term you might not be able to do some of your favourite things, like reading, watching TV and doing sports. Granted sports is a team activity normally but you get my point, use the Christmas break as a chance for you to do what you enjoy.

Personally, in my Christmas Break I'll be enjoying myself and relaxing by seeing my friends and family and catching up on anything that I've been meaning to do but haven't gone round to it yet. Like, watching some films I've recorded six months ago.

Catch-Up:

If you're a bit behind with your university reading, coursework or anything else, the Christmas break is a perfect time to catch up because it's four weeks of no lectures, no assignments and no readings. Meaning you can spend at least some of that time catching up with all of your work.

As a result of nothing is worse than going into a new term that brings more readings, more lectures and more everything, and you're still playing catch-up with last term's stuff. This isn't fun and it will lead to burn out.

It's that simple.

Therefore, if you are behind, I know a number of students that spend the first week of the Christmas break catching up with their work so they had the rest of the break to enjoy themselves.

So you might want to try that.

Personally, I've always used the breaks as deadlines and I make sure I'd finished all my work before then, but I know students aren't always able to do that.

Work:

Let's face it, university is expensive!

Therefore, during the Christmas Break, you might want to work, do some extra shifts or take a Christmas temporary job for the season. Not only will it give you some extra money to spend (or save), it will also allow you to gain new skills, experience and meet new people.

If you are going to seek out a Christmas temporary job I would recommend you start looking for that in early October or right NOW if it's later. I've never done this sort of thing so I cannot comment on it too much, but it is an idea if you want some extra money.

Conclusion: Maintaining A Good Work-Life Balance

Throughout the blog post I have mentioned I lot of different ideas, from relaxing to catching up to working. But if you take anything away from this blog post, please let it be this, whatever you decide to do during your Christmas break, you need to maintain a good work-life balance.

If you don't then you will most probably burn out, decrease your mental health and wellbeing. No one wants that.

Therefore, if you are going to work a job or work on catching up with your university work, then make sure you schedule some time for yourself, your friends and your family. Everything in life is about balance so please keep your time balanced to protect yourself.

In my Christmas break, I'll be doing a few things that most people consider "work" but I will still be spending a lot of time with friends and family because I know the balance, and its importance.

All in all, have fun, have an amazing break and find a balance. You'll be thanking me afterwards.

HOW TO FACE THE NEW YEAR FOR UNIVERSITY STUDENTS?

I think we've all had an experience at university when it comes to the New Year and we slightly (or completely) feel uninterested in university.

In case this happens to you, definitely keep reading because this chapter is designed to help you. And even if you don't believe you suffer from this, still read it because it might make you really excited about getting back to university.

How To Face The New Year For University Students?

Continuing on with our look at the Christmas Break at university, we need to start looking at this new year we all find ourselves in because it can both positively and negatively affect university. As sometimes after the long, wonderful Christmas Break, we struggle to get back into the university swing of things.

Therefore, whilst we'll look at the *getting back into*

the swing of things in the next blog post, we need to take a step back and think about the new year from a mindset perspective.

Why Do We Need To Face The New Year?

For lots of people the new year is an amazing time, it's a time of new beginning, new years resolutions and starting new hobbies or interests that we want to explore.

Personally, I love the New Year because it means I can start new creative projects, new amazing new modules at university and explore new areas. For example, in 2022 on my podcast I'll be exploring the topics of Dementia and Male Suicide more depth.

However, when it comes to university, the new year can be a dreaded reminder that we need to go back there, away from our family and friends and back into the so-called grind of everyday university life. Including the typical cycle of lectures, reading, assignments, repeat.

In case you're one of these students who isn't looking forward to the New Year of university, this post is designed to help you.

Even if you are looking forward to the new year, this should still be useful.

New Modules

Something I always love about the start of any new term is the starting of new modules because some of them are amazing. For example, in my second year of university, I had my personality psychology and social psychology of the individual modules starting in the new year. Both of these modules were brilliant and I loved them because they were great fun and extremely interesting.

Therefore, if you find yourself not able to face the new year at university, look at your timetable (Active Class can help with this) and think about what modules you have coming up. That alone will probably give you something to look forward to and perhaps get excited about.

In addition, I should note that even if you have a module that you are not looking forward to, still look forward to it because you might love it.

This happened to be in my second year because I was not looking forward to personality psychology in the slightest. But as I mentioned earlier, it turned out to be one of my favourite modules and something I will continue to learn about independently in the coming years.

All in all, look at what modules you have in the new year and focus on them. Some of them will be exciting and focus on them. This is especially true if you've picked a degree topic you love.

Returning To University Friends and Activities

Perhaps one of the biggest reasons to get excited and face the new year is that you'll be returning to university so you can see friends and do your university activities again. I'm sure this means clubbing and partying for some people and that's fine.

Yet for others this can be catching up, going out with friends and attending the university socials again.

All three of them is definitely why I'm looking forward to the new year.

Additionally, I know other countries don't have Societies (social clubs for adults basically) like we do in the UK, but this is another reason to face the new year. You can return to university and see everyone in the society again.

For me it was great to see all the different people from baking society again after the Christmas Break in my first year.

Overall, if you can't face the new year, don't focus on the learning part of university. Focus on the opportunity to see friends again, catch up and do activities.

Short and Long Term

If any of the above hasn't helped you face the new year then maybe a completely different way of looking at the new year will help you. Try to look at the new year in terms of your short term and long term gains.

For instance, in the short term, the amazing new year at university will give you opportunities to learn, grow as a person and meet new wonderful people. Then in the long term will could help you to get higher grades, help you with postgraduate applications and get a better job.

Or most importantly facing the new year at university will help you have fun at university. Since many students love university because it provides a great environment to explore topics, make friends and do things you wouldn't normally do that the "real world" doesn't allow you to do.

<u>Conclusion:</u>

So what I'm trying to say is, is the new year is NOT a time to dread because you need to go back to university and re-enter the so-called grind of lectures, reading, assignments, repeat.

Instead I really want you to see the new year as just that. A new beginning, a beginning to a time filled with new learning opportunities, chances to catch up with friends, do social activities with them again and a beginning that will help you in the long term.

I love the new year and I hope that you're looking forward to the new year too.

Go and make the most of it!

HOW TO GET BACK INTO THE SWING OF THINGS AT UNIVERSITY?

To wrap up this section of the book and before we move onto our final section on a personal favourite of mine, we need to look at getting back into the swing of things.

Due to without fail and I really have tried to find a university student that doesn't fall into this, but whenever we get back from a break. It always take a bit of time for us to get back into the swing of university life.

This chapter is designed to help all of us get back into the swing of things a bit faster. This is even more useful if you have an exam or coursework due it shortly after you return to university.

<u>How To Get Back In The Swing of Things For University Students?</u>

To conclude this mini-series looking at the university Christmas break, we need to look at returning to university. Since the Christmas break is basically four weeks off for us and we get to do what we want, when we want without having to do any reading, assignments or lectures. But four weeks is a long time so when it comes to returning to university it can take some people a while to get back in the swing of things. Therefore, this blog post is designed to help you speed up the process a bit.

Plan Effectively

The major tip I have for you is to plan your time effective like you normally (should) do, because planning will allow you to see what you have to do, when you're going to do so it doesn't stress you out.

No one wants this on the first week back at university, so check your timetable and module pages to see what you need to do and plan your time effectively.

In addition, it's worth noting that the first week back everyone is getting back into the swing of things so the first week can be rather easy. Especially as new modules tend to have the introduction that first week, so that's one less thing to be stressed out about.

In my experience, I can't remember a busy first week back in my other university years, as both years I always had new modules with the introductions.

Just Relax

As I wrote the last section I was reminded of this pathological fear or hurry that every student seems to be in when they return to university after any break. Lots of students fear they'll need to hit the ground running, they have tons to do and they won't have any adjustment time.

I'm sure that is true for some students, but the vast majority?

No.

As a result of the way how the vast majority of modules work is they introduce you to the topic in the first week, then they progress through the topics. Then if there's an essay, assignment or any coursework for the module that tends to be given out in the middle of the term so it can be handed in towards the end.

What I'm trying to say is, there is no reason for modules to get busy in the first few weeks of term, so you shouldn't have to hit the ground running when you return.

All in all, my unofficial advice would be to just relax, all the concerns, anxiety and even fears you have about returning to university are just in your head. If you relax, look forward to going back and realise you shouldn't have tons of work to do the second you go back. You should be able to get back in the swing of things easily.

Don't Hang Onto Your Christmas Break Routine:

The later wake-up times, the lack of readings and everything else can seen amazing to lots of students so they can want to hang onto those blissful moments from their Christmas break.

Whilst I can't relate to blissful unproductive moments or late sleeping ins, I do understand people wanting to hang onto some of those habits from their break. Most people love sleeping in, not having to worry about doing x, y and z, but if the hanging on to these habits is preventing you from getting back into the swing of university, don't you think they need to go?

Instead of longing for a later wake-up time and not doing readings, lectures and more, maybe trying to throw yourself back into university life might help you. I'm not just talking about the reading and other learning aspects of university, I'm talking about the social side too.

Throwing yourself into socials, catching up with friends and going to Societies you're a part of might be what you need to get back into the swing of things.

Once you remember how great your university social (and learning, perhaps?) life was, you should see that getting back into university life is the best thing for you.

Conclusion:

To wrap up this blog then the series, I know that returning to university can seem hard at times. Especially when you've come back from a brilliant 4 weeks off without any of the pressure or things to do from university. Therefore, it can make getting back into the swing of things hard for all of us, but I now hope that this blog post has helped you realise why you need to get back into the swing of things and how to do it.

In terms of the series, I love Christmas, the break it provides and what that break allows me to do as a person. It's a great time for students and I hope after reading this series you now know how to prepare yourself for the last week, the break itself, returning in the new year and how to get back into the swing of university life.

As I always say nothing about university is meant to be hard, difficult or boring, both in terms of the learning, assignments and more. It's all about mindset which is was a lot of this series was about.

So I hope you enjoyed your break, return to university and I wish you the best for the new year.

PART SIX: PLACEMENTS, WORK EXPEREINCE AND SUMMER HOLIDAYS

HOW TO MAKE THE MOST OF YOUR SUMMER HOLIDAYS FOR UNIVERSITY STUDENTS?

The final section of the book could possibly be one of the most important in the entire book because learning, academic and the like is critical at university. But your employability is something else that is absolutely critical because at the end of the day, your degree is great and very valuable but it is your extra things that help you to stand out in the job market.

That's why this next section will focus on things like getting work experience, placement years, a part-time job and more.

So I cannot stress enough the importance of reading this next section and it is probably a great idea to actually implement and try out some of these chapters.

How To Make The Most Of Your Summer Holidays For University Students?

The summer holidays are a great time of the year. No stress of exams, university or coursework deadlines. After a hard year at university, we finally get to do whatever we want.

But how do we make the most of it?

That's the focus of today's post by looking at relaxation tips, work experience and volunteering.

Relaxation

At first, I was going to try and find out some psychology articles on relaxation, but they're complex!

But relaxation is so important in the summer holidays because you need to allow yourself time to destress and (basically) recover after the academic year. Because being a university student is just like being a full-time employee. You have deadlines, full days most days and you have to do lots of reading and learning. (But you don't get paid!)

Additionally, it is critical for you to relax and enjoy your time off so you can maintain a healthy work-life balance and, most importantly, so you don't decrease your mental health.

Therefore, do what you love during the summer holidays. Be it going out with friends and family, reading books, going on holiday. Do whatever you need to do to relax.

Personally, I enjoy reading and spending time with friends and family so I do that to relax.

Work Experience

Despite relaxing being important in the summer holidays, spending three months doing nothing else. Could be seen as not a good use of your time?

This is why lots of students tend to get part-time

jobs and try to get work experience in their chosen field.

Getting work experience for a few months does have a lot of benefits. For example, it gives you a chance to develop your skills for future employment and this will increase your employability. Since employers are always looking for people who have experience.

In addition, if you can get work experience in your chosen field then this will almost certainly help you in the future. Because it will help you stand out from the crowd.

For example, I'm doing a psychology degree but so are thousands of other people. Therefore, when I finish my degree and complete my Masters too. Then I will be just another psychology graduate.

This is why getting work experience is critical because it allows you to stand out from the crowd. Which is why I chose a psychology degree with a year of work experience included.

Overall, you can help make the most of your summer holidays by trying to get work experience, and most (if not all) universities have an employability service or job shop to help you find and get experience.

<u>Volunteering</u>

Building upon the idea of experience, volunteering is another great way to make the most of your summer holidays.

Since volunteering isn't only a great addition to your CV. Helping you stand out in the job market because volunteering can help you with people skills, confidence amongst other needed skills. But it can help you meet new people and most importantly make a difference.

Also, with the Internet at our fingertips, it's easier than ever before to find volunteering opportunities. As well as most universities have a good volunteering scheme or group to help you find opportunities.

For example, my university has opportunities with the homeless, woodlands, nature and lots of other opportunities.

And you don't need to volunteer for tens of hours a week. Two or three hours is plenty and it's better than nothing.

This all comes back to balance and moderation. You don't want to burn out with volunteering work.

<u>Conclusion:</u>

I really hope you enjoyed today's blog post and I really do encourage you to make the most of your summer holidays. Sadly, us university students don't have a lot of them left before we enter the real world (scary!) so it is important to make good use of them.

So please do relax but think about looking for work experience and volunteering opportunities too. You can develop lots of great skills by doing this.

Have a great day!

HOW TO FIND A PART-TIME JOB AT UNIVERSITY?

When it comes to university, we all want a part-time job and they can be extremely useful. They can help us cover our bills and help us to have a bit of extra money in your pocket, but there are plenty of words of caution to.

Thankfully this chapter covers it all, or the vast majority of it anyway, so before you get a part-time job at university definitely read this chapter.

<u>How To Find A Part-Time Job At University?</u>

When you go to university, it can be very handy to have a part time job during university because it allows you to increase your employability, earns you a bit of money (which is always great) and it allows you to mix with people you might never have met otherwise. Therefore, in this blog post I'm going to be giving you some tips to finding a part-time job, and some important things to think about too.

Word Of Caution On Part-Time Jobs:

Before we dive into how to find a job at university, I have to mention that you need to consider the hours you can do. Since I remember from my first year, my flatmates were all very excited to get part-time work during their studying then they quickly realised they were in an awful situation. They were working lots of long hours and they didn't have enough time to study, but they couldn't reduce their hours, because their bosses didn't see the problem.

Therefore, my suggestion is before you set out to find a part-time job, take a look at your timetable and see how many hours you can work without it impacting your studies.

I think I remember a university person saying to us, *we advise you only do 20 hours or less a week*. In all honesty, this makes perfect sense, because 20 hours is still a good amount of work to earn you some money, but it isn't so much that it should impact your studies.

So 20 hours or less might be the way to go. Personally I would stick with less if you can.

How To Find A Part-Time Job At University?
The University Itself:

Now universities make great use of students in their labour force because there are so many jobs available to students at the start of the academic year. Since all the cafes, libraries and whatever else your university has all need to be filled with student workers. Even more so because each year the final year students leave the university so these places need to be restocked with new student staff members.

Also for the more graduate-level students, you might want to check out if your university allows you to do some teachings (I imagine they all do). For example, the very good editor of this blog does some teaching as he's a PhD student.

As a result, when it comes to finding jobs at university, it is a great idea to look at the different places at your university online to see if they have any jobs. For example, I know if I go onto any bar, café or restaurant website that's at my university, there will always be a job section at the bottom.

The key to finding jobs is just having a look and trying to make the most of it.

A Job Shop?

Of course all of these blog posts are just my experiences and thoughts, but at my university they have A Job Shop. I'm sure other universities will have something similar so it's good to be aware of.

This Job Shop is where the university, local businesses and other places advertise their jobs to students. Making this a great place to have a look if you're looking for work.

Also it's worth noting that universities do Career Fairs where hundreds of companies come in and try to sell themselves to the students. They can actually be quite good (Just don't do what I do and just go for the freebies).

Online:

Stepping away from the university-centric ways

of finding jobs, you can always look online. Each country will have their own job seeking platforms, like Indeed in the UK, and these are effective ways to find work. You tend to just search for a job, filter the results by part-time work and apply for a job that way.

<u>Conclusion:</u>

Whenever you start thinking about getting a part-time job at university, it can be daunting because you don't know where to look. But hopefully after reading this post, you now have some idea about how to find one. Whether it is at the university itself, a job shop or online, there are plenty of ways to find a job.

But please, remember to prioritise your degree because that is why you are there in the first place.

And you never know, your degree job could or should pay you a lot more than your part-time job, so why wouldn't you focus on the degree?

HOW DOES WORK EXPEREINCE BENEFIT UNIVERSITY STUDENTS?

When it comes to employability and getting work experience lots of students don't see the point in it, so this next chapter focuses on the 5 main benefits of work experience and why students really need to do it.

You'll be surprised at the amazing benefits doing some work experience can have, so definitely check out this next chapter.

How Does Work Experience Benefit University Students?

In this increasingly competitive world, it is becoming harder to stand out in the job market and this is where work experience comes in. Because employers generally prefer people to have experience when they apply for jobs. So, it's important to consider How Does Work Experience Benefit University Students?

5 Benefits of University Work Experience

Taste of A Future Career

One of the many reasons why I picked to do a placement year (year of work experience) was because I wanted to explore what it was like to work in psychology. Therefore, I'm working with a great team in September 2021 to conduct some research.

This will allow me to see if I enjoy and I can see myself working in research for the rest of my life.

Personally, I would prefer to find out what I don't like about working in psychology now, compared to finding out after I've found a *proper* job that I hate it.

Overall, this is one reason why work experience is great to do because it allows you to see what you want to do in the future. Because you might find out you thought you loved Clinical practice, but after your work experience you realise you hate it.

Learn Beyond The Classroom

As great as lectures and textbooks are, they can only teach you so much. The rest of the skills you need you have to learn in the real world, and you can't do that without experiencing your degree in the real world.

Therefore, work experience is great for allowing you to develop skills you learn about in the classroom, but you don't get to apply.

Another point to add is in textbooks, they can describe a particular skill but it isn't until you have to use it in the real world that you realise how the skill actually works.

For example, in clinical psychology, we're told a lot about active listening and it sounds easy enough. But in the real world it isn't as easy as it sounds.

Meaning experience can help you familiarise yourself with how your degree works in the real world. Sometimes this can surprise you because the theory says one thing, your experience says another. But isn't that the fun of learning?

On the whole, getting work experience is great because it allows you to develop the skills you learn about in the classroom and turn the theory into practical knowledge.

Being Paid Is A Good Feeling:

Whilst this doesn't apply to all work experience because when I was applying to my placement there weren't many paid placements and generally work experience is unpaid. But I don't mind that necessarily because my thinking is if I get the experience now then this makes me more employable in the future. Meaning I'll hopefully make more money in the long term.

Of course, your circumstances might be different and I'm fairly sure if you hunted high and low you might be able to find some paid work experience.

However, if you do get paid work experience, this can be a great feeling as it allows you to work in the field you love, get the other benefits we've discussed, and you get to make some money too. Which is always good!

<u>Increased Employability</u>

Our final point we've preluded to throughout this blog post but I want to say it explicitly- work experience can equip you with skills and experiences that lots of people don't have.

For example, my placement year in research will help me develop my skills in researching a real-world setting. Other students in my year they'll have research experience from their degree but not necessarily in a real-life setting.

If you studied medicine and you got work experience at a Doctor's Surgery, you would have real-world experience and skills that I don't think many other students would have.

Overall, work experience can be great for increasing your employability because you will have some great skills and experiences that you can draw on in your future work.

Conclusion:

Whether you're actively looking for work experience or you're just interested in the idea, I hope you've found this useful. Work experience can have some great benefits from skill development to learning new things to increasing your employability. I hoped you learnt something.

Have a great day!

SHOULD YOU DO A PLACEMENT YEAR FOR UNIVERSITY STUDENTS?

For the final chapter of this book, we're going to briefly look at an area that is close to my heart. Whilst I have an entire book on psychology placements, why they're great and what I did during it. I want to introduce you to this great area of work experience and practical experience that can really help you to increase your employability as part of your degree.

I love this area and I really hope you will too.

Should You Do a Placement Year For University Students?

Some courses offer these things call 'Placement years' and lots of university students have an idea about what they are, but they don't know why they should do one or if it's even right for them. In this blog post, we're going to explore this great (and very fun) topic because it can help you a lot in the future.

Firstly, a placement year is when you do a year of work experience whilst you're still at university between your second and final year. If you google placement year you'll get lots of horrible definitions but this is a great definition for this blog post.

Let's focus on Should You Do A Placement Year?

Address The Options

I first heard of a placement year when I was visiting the University of Bath in 2018 because the guiders were trying to promote the placement year course to us. This made me very hooked on the idea of a placement for reasons you'll see later on.

After this, I began to explore various psychology courses with placement years because I wanted the work experience. But so few universities offer placement years. Some degrees don't offer it.

Therefore, when you're thinking about should you do a placement year, you need to look at your options in a few ways. For example, does your degree offer the opportunity for placements?

Note: if you're degree or field doesn't offer placements then you can still get work and practical experience by looking for volunteering and work experience opportunities. As discussed a few blog posts ago.

Another important aspect to consider is, is your placement year at a university you would want to go to?

Thankfully, I was lucky enough because for psychology placements I had the opportunity of the University of Bath and the University of Kent. I'm glad my choice was made for me because I didn't get into Bath, but if I was given the choice. I would need to think about what university I would prefer and I would be happier in.

Overall, when considering should you do a placement year, I highly recommend you look at your options and see what's right for you.

<u>Advantages and Disadvantages</u>

So if a placement year is a possibility for you, what are the advantages and disadvantages?

The main two advantages are very simple and powerful.

Firstly, a placement year will give you great work experience for your future career in your field. Making you're more employable to companies because unlike the thousands of graduates with their shiny new degree. You'll actually have a degree AND work experience.

Secondly, as I mentioned in the last blog post, you'll develop amazing skills and experiences that university doesn't teach you. Allowing you to increase your knowledge beyond the classroom.

However, like everything in life, there are always disadvantages and again I believe there are two main ones.

The first being you getting your undergraduate degree will be delayed by a year. Meaning when you start your final university year you're friends and other people who didn't do a placement year will be gone.

This was something I was concerned about a few months ago when I realised it. But I always have a long term focus so yes this is a disadvantage now but the placement will still benefit me in the future.

In addition, we live in a modern, technological world so you can always keep in touch and talk to them over the phone, text or whatever the next big *cool* kid thing is.

Finally, I think the last disadvantage would technically be the so-called administration fee which is the technical term for why you still have to pay reduced tuition fees during your placement year. Me and my friends at my University Outreach department couldn't get our heads around that.

Anyway, whilst I'm going to be focusing on the UK here, it's still useful for all readers. You will probably still have to apply for your maintenance loan and tuition fees from Student Finance England. As I always say when I'm helping to give a student finance presentation to secondary schools, this extra debt isn't as scary as it sounds and a placement year could help you make more money in the long term.

Note: of course, it is a bit more complicated than that and this post is not financial or official advice.

<u>Is It Right For You?</u>

As much as I would love to give you a definitive answer, I can't.

The university degree you pick is a very personal choice, but I hope after reading this post. You're at least more aware of the benefits and drawbacks of getting a placement year.

The only other thing I will say is most

universities that offer a placement year with a course will consider offering you a place on the normal degree without the placement. If they reject you for the placement year.

At the end of the day, you need to do what's right for you and your life.

Thank you for reading and have a great day!

CONCLUSION

To finish up this book I really hope that that you have found this useful as we have looked at a lot of different bits and pieces. As well as whilst this was definitely more of a scattergun book to some extent, in terms of we looked at a wide range of things. I still hope it was useful.

Personally I still really wished that I had a book or resource like this back when I was starting university. Since it would have been great to know more about work experience, getting a part-time job and all the information about exams.

In addition, whilst tons of people don't really talk about the topics included in this book, they are still so important to being successful and enjoying your time at university.

Also as someone who is actually an introvert by nature, I want to say that for all my fellow introverts, university can still be great fun where you made lots of friends and have a great time.

Of course, you do NOT need to go to tons of loud clubs, parties and the like, but as this book has shown you there are still plenty of ways to make friends, have fun all whilst studying for exams and coursework as well.

Next Steps

Personally, as these books are useful university guides, I always like to end them by suggesting a few unofficial steps to help you further. So just like the other books in the series, I have three to share with you.

Firstly, I highly recommend that you do implement some of the chapters in the book. Be it the chapters from the social tip section, exam or coursework section. Just please make sure you actually do take some of this information onboard as it will really help you in your university journey.

Secondly, definitely check out the other two books in the series *University Mental Health and Mindset* and *How Does University Work?* Both of these are really interesting, engaging books that will help you learn even more about university. As well as both of them are filled with additional tips for university life.

In addition, they're available from wherever you bought this book from.

Finally, as this book is mainly for university psychology students. Then I highly recommend you check out my other psychology books at www.connorwhiteley.net/books

As at this point, we have covered a lot of

different topics in the books, and lots of people have found them useful and interesting, including graduate students.

Furthermore, I highly recommend that you check out The Psychology World Podcast, available on all major podcast apps and YouTube, as we're covering fascinating topics that you are rarely taught in textbooks and the lecture theatre so if you want to deepen your psychology knowledge, those two tips I highly recommend.

However, I want to leave you by reminding you that the entire purpose of university isn't just to learn. But it's to have fun too.

Just remember that and you should be fine.

 **GET YOUR EXCLUSIVE FREE 8 BOOK PSYCHOLOGY BOXSET AND YOUR EMAIL PSYCHOLOGY COURSE HERE!**

https://www.subscribepage.com/psychologyboxset

Thank you for reading.
I hoped you enjoyed it.
If you want a FREE book and keep up to date about new books and project. Then please sign up for my newsletter at www.connorwhiteley.net/
Have a great day.

CHECK OUT THE PSYCHOLOGY WORLD PODCAST FOR MORE PSYCHOLOGY INFORMATION!
AVAILABLE ON ALL MAJOR PODCAST APPS.

About the author:

Connor Whiteley is the author of over 60 books in the sci-fi fantasy, nonfiction psychology and books for writer's genre and he is a Human Branding Speaker and Consultant.

He is a passionate warhammer 40,000 reader, psychology student and author.

Who narrates his own audiobooks and he hosts The Psychology World Podcast.

All whilst studying Psychology at the University of Kent, England.

Also, he was a former Explorer Scout where he gave a speech to the Maltese President in August 2018 and he attended Prince Charles' 70th Birthday Party at Buckingham Palace in May 2018.

Plus, he is a self-confessed coffee lover!

All books in 'An Introductory Series':

BIOLOGICAL PSYCHOLOGY 3RD EDITION
COGNITIVE PSYCHOLOGY THIRD EDITION
SOCIAL PSYCHOLOGY- 3RD EDITION
ABNORMAL PSYCHOLOGY 3RD EDITION
PSYCHOLOGY OF RELATIONSHIPS- 3RD EDITION
DEVELOPMENTAL PSYCHOLOGY 3RD EDITION
HEALTH PSYCHOLOGY
RESEARCH IN PSYCHOLOGY
A GUIDE TO MENTAL HEALTH AND TREATMENT AROUND THE WORLD- A GLOBAL LOOK AT DEPRESSION
FORENSIC PSYCHOLOGY
THE FORENSIC PSYCHOLOGY OF THEFT, BURGLARY AND OTHER CRIMES AGAINST PROPERTY
CRIMINAL PROFILING: A FORENSIC PSYCHOLOGY GUIDE TO FBI PROFILING AND GEOGRAPHICAL AND STATISTICAL PROFILING.
CLINICAL PSYCHOLOGY
FORMULATION IN PSYCHOTHERAPY
PERSONALITY PSYCHOLOGY AND INDIVIDUAL DIFFERENCES
CLINICAL PSYCHOLOGY REFLECTIONS VOLUME 1
CLINICAL PSYCHOLOGY REFLECTIONS VOLUME 2

CULT PSYCHOLOGY
Police Psychology

A Psychology Student's Guide To University
How Does University Work?
A Student's Guide To University And Learning
University Mental Health and Mindset

Companion guides:
BIOLOGICAL PSYCHOLOGY 2ND EDITION WORKBOOK
COGNITIVE PSYCHOLOGY 2ND EDITION WORKBOOK
SOCIOCULTURAL PSYCHOLOGY 2ND EDITION WORKBOOK
ABNORMAL PSYCHOLOGY 2ND EDITION WORKBOOK
PSYCHOLOGY OF HUMAN RELATIONSHIPS 2ND EDITION WORKBOOK
HEALTH PSYCHOLOGY WORKBOOK
FORENSIC PSYCHOLOGY WORKBOOK

OTHER SHORT STORIES BY CONNOR WHITELEY

<u>Mystery Short Stories:</u>
Poison In The Candy Cane
Christmas Innocence
You Better Watch Out
Christmas Theft
Trouble In Christmas
Smell of The Lake
Problem In A Car
Theft, Past and Team
Embezzler In The Room
A Strange Way To Go
A Horrible Way To Go
Ann Awful Way To Go
An Old Way To Go
A Fishy Way To Go
A Pointy Way To Go
A High Way To Go
A Fiery Way To Go
A Glassy Way To Go
A Chocolatey Way To Go
Kendra Detective Mystery Collection Volume 1
Kendra Detective Mystery Collection Volume 2
Stealing A Chance At Freedom
Glassblowing and Death
Theft of Independence
Cookie Thief
Marble Thief
Book Thief

Art Thief
Mated At The Morgue
The Big Five Whoopee Moments
Stealing An Election
Mystery Short Story Collection Volume 1
Mystery Short Story Collection Volume 2

Science Fiction Short Stories:
The First Rememberer
Life of A Rememberer
System of Wonder
Lifesaver
Remarkable Way She Died
The Interrogation of Annabella Stormic
Blade of The Emperor
Arbiter's Truth
Computation of Battle
Old One's Wrath
Puppets and Masters
Ship of Plague
Interrogation
Edge of Failure
One Way Choice
Acceptable Losses
Balance of Power
Good Idea At The Time
Escape Plan
Escape In The Hesitation
Inspiration In Need
Singing Warriors

Knowledge is Power
Killer of Polluters
Climate of Death
The Family Mailing Affair
Defining Criminality
The Martian Affair
A Cheating Affair
The Little Café Affair
Mountain of Death
Prisoner's Fight
Claws of Death
Bitter Air
Honey Hunt
Blade On A Train

<u>Fantasy Short Stories:</u>
City of Snow
City of Light
City of Vengeance
Dragons, Goats and Kingdom
Smog The Pathetic Dragon
Don't Go In The Shed
The Tomato Saver
The Remarkable Way She Died
The Bloodied Rose
Asmodia's Wrath
Heart of A Killer
Emissary of Blood
Dragon Coins
Dragon Tea

Dragon Rider
Sacrifice of the Soul
Heart of The Flesheater
Heart of The Regent
Heart of The Standing
Feline of The Lost
Heart of The Story
City of Fire
Awaiting Death

Other books by Connor Whiteley:

<u>Bettie English Private Eye Series</u>
A Very Private Woman
The Russian Case
A Very Urgent Matter
A Case Most Personal
Trains, Scots and Private Eyes
The Federation Protects

<u>The Fireheart Fantasy Series</u>
Heart of Fire
Heart of Lies
Heart of Prophecy
Heart of Bones
Heart of Fate

<u>City of Assassins (Urban Fantasy)</u>
City of Death
City of Marytrs
City of Pleasure
City of Power

<u>Agents of The Emperor</u>
Return of The Ancient Ones
Vigilance
Angels of Fire
Kingmaker
<u>The Garro Series- Fantasy/Sci-fi</u>
GARRO: GALAXY'S END
GARRO: RISE OF THE ORDER

GARRO: END TIMES
GARRO: SHORT STORIES
GARRO: COLLECTION
GARRO: HERESY
GARRO: FAITHLESS
GARRO: DESTROYER OF WORLDS
GARRO: COLLECTIONS BOOK 4-6
GARRO: MISTRESS OF BLOOD
GARRO: BEACON OF HOPE
GARRO: END OF DAYS

Winter Series- Fantasy Trilogy Books
WINTER'S COMING
WINTER'S HUNT
WINTER'S REVENGE
WINTER'S DISSENSION

Miscellaneous:
RETURN
FREEDOM
SALVATION
Reflection of Mount Flame
The Masked One
The Great Deer

Audiobooks by Connor Whiteley:
BIOLOGICAL PSYCHOLOGY
COGNITIVE PSYCHOLOGY
SOCIOCULTURAL PSYCHOLOGY
ABNORMAL PSYCHOLOGY
PSYCHOLOGY OF HUMAN RELATIONSHIPS
HEALTH PSYCHOLOGY
DEVELOPMENTAL PSYCHOLOGY
RESEARCH IN PSYCHOLOGY
FORENSIC PSYCHOLOGY
GARRO: GALAXY'S END
GARRO: RISE OF THE ORDER
GARRO: SHORT STORIES
GARRO: END TIMES
GARRO: COLLECTION
GARRO: HERESY
GARRO: FAITHLESS
GARRO: DESTROYER OF WORLDS
GARRO: COLLECTION BOOKS 4-6
GARRO: COLLECTION BOOKS 1-6

Business books:
TIME MANAGEMENT: A GUIDE FOR STUDENTS AND WORKERS
LEADERSHIP: WHAT MAKES A GOOD LEADER? A GUIDE FOR STUDENTS AND WORKERS.
BUSINESS SKILLS: HOW TO SURVIVE THE BUSINESS WORLD? A GUIDE FOR STUDENTS, EMPLOYEES AND EMPLOYERS.
BUSINESS COLLECTION

GET YOUR FREE BOOK AT:
WWW.CONNORWHITELEY.NET

www.ingramcontent.com/pod-product-compliance
Lightning Source LLC
LaVergne TN
LVHW011835060526
838200LV00053B/4031